Our *Ben* and *Us*

Our Ben and Us

CLIVE HISCOX

Library of Congress Control Number:		2017908359
ISBN:	Hardcover	978-1-5434-8570-7
	Softcover	978-1-5434-8569-1
	eBook	978-1-5434-8568-4

Print information available on the last page.

Rev. date: 07/10/2017

To order additional copies of this book, contact:
Xlibris
800-056-3182
www.Xlibrispublishing.co.uk
Orders@Xlibrispublishing.co.uk
759962

FOREWORD

I t's only fair to start by saying that I never met or knew Ben Hiscox. I hope I can explain why that doesn't matter too much.

I'm sure we may have shaken hands, drank a drink in the same place, nodded at each other as we passed by or maybe had a chat in the way you do with people in your "circle". Those you kind of know, but just haven't had the chance to make friends with yet.

Reflecting now on Ben's tragic and untimely death in March 2015, three things occur to me.

Firstly, the fact I never had the chance to become friendly with someone like Ben is entirely my loss.

Secondly he had, and has, more friends and loved ones than anyone I think I've ever known, without needing to add me to the ranks.

Lastly, had I had been lucky enough to be part of that group, God only knows what capers, pranks and experiences a friend like Ben would have led a beer-loving, easily influenced, "'wannabe one of the lads" like me into! I fear he would have had me for breakfast, lunch, dinner and several brandies and cigars afterwards!

One of Ben's many passions was Bristol Rovers Football Club.

It's been an honour and a privilege to have worked as a volunteer for The Gas for almost 25 years, with 22 of them as stadium announcer. At 23 years of age, I started as understudy to the legendary and infamous

Keith Valle – and for a Gashead who cut his teeth on the Popular Side at Twerton Park, purely by chance I landed a life-changing dream job as PA announcer for our beloved football club.

The biggest privilege in this role is to meet so many like-minded people. One big family or fraternity, you might say. I never underestimate how much it means to supporters who may have their birthday or other celebrations read out in front of thousands of people over the (often patchy!) PA system. We've had pitch-side proposals, presentations to superstars and many a footballing legend amongst us alongside the 90 minutes of football we all come to watch.

There is another side to the job. Like all families, sometimes we lose loved ones. I get many requests to read obituaries for Rovers fans that have passed away. These are always difficult because, in what is effectively a cauldron of footballing passion and fever, people are in pain at the game without much-missed loved ones.

In my 20-odd years as master of ceremonies as I guess some would call it, some of the most difficult of these occasions have been people I have known. Again, maybe not friends in the true sense of the word, but all part of our Rovers family.

Writing this, I particularly remember the passing of great men like Denis Dunford and Ray Kendall – Bristol Rovers legends who became friends and colleagues. Of course, people like this are given a full tribute with either a minute's silence or applause, only ever reserved for dignitaries of our football club.

In my role at the Rovers, I have met wonderful people and formed what I know will be lifelong friendships. One of those friends is Rick Johansen, a Stoke Gifford villager who told me about Ben and his tragic accident.

Death never comes easy, but when it happens to a young man, a lad in his prime playing the game he and we all love, in a million-to-one chance, it becomes beyond human comprehension.

Rick invited me to the village to meet some of Ben's friends, teammates and family and I was absolutely blown backwards by the shock, grief and tributes – but most of all by the incredible outpouring of love following Ben's loss. This community, in this great city of Bristol, was as one mourning a young man who clearly had touched so many lives.

To their eternal credit, and in no small way influenced by the wave of emotion and support that swept across the entire city – red or blue and white – the board of Bristol Rovers sanctioned a minute's applause at the next home game, Good Friday if I recall.

I refer back to the fact that a tribute on this scale is usually reserved for ex-players, directors or VIPs like the lovely men that were Denis Dunford and Ray Kendall.

I mention Ben in the same breath as Denis and Ray as, although I have addressed a silent stadium on many occasions for tragedies or tributes to loved ones, these were the three occasions when I had to physically overcome emotion and tears and do my best to get some words out that did justice to their loss. I did my best. I hope it was enough.

That day, I met Ben's parents Clive and Gloria. I realised that, although I didn't "know" them, I recognised them straight away. They are lovely, lovely people. They are part of our family – as was Ben. The Bristol Rovers family.

Clive's outpouring of grief and gratitude during the applause set the stadium alight. Gloria's dignity shone through. Ben's friends and teammates didn't hide their tears or grief and were a credit to this immense man, their great friend.

I don't feel deserving or qualified to write the foreword to what you will now read is a wonderful tribute to a much-loved son.

Nevertherless, I am honoured to have been asked.

Sleep peacefully Ben and, for all of you reading, give an extra hug or kiss to all those people around you that you love.

Nick Day
Bristol Rovers FC

CONTENTS

INTRODUCTION

Never in my wildest dreams did I ever envisage writing a book, let alone writing it in the circumstances I find myself in. It has been like a journey – one I could never have imagined, yet one during which I have learned many things.

I believe we are all blessed with certain qualities – some that we may not even be aware of. In my case, to my surprise, it has been my memory that has served me well just when I needed it most.

From their teens right up to now, two of my nephews always maintained that I am just like a kid. Lee and Wayne always had smiles on their faces as they said this, but now I can see exactly why they came to this conclusion. I'm afraid it's something that just comes naturally. It's part of my make up so it's a bit late to try and change it now.

Everything I have written in this book is true and exactly how I saw things through my own eyes. I am grateful to others for providing their input on how they saw things through their eyes. I hope I have managed to describe each episode in a manner which brings a smile to your face.

The title of this book is based on a huge character and primarily his family, although if I am totally honest, the term *us* represents so many friends of all ages whose acquaintance has been shared over a period of time. That friendship often made him part of their family, so all those people come under the category *us*.

I have portrayed much of our own family life and family members in the hope that the reader can imagine the scenes, situations, and the individual characters, hopefully helping to build a picture as the storyline develops.

The great game of football plays a fair part in my story, although there is much more to it than that. I commend all true and loyal football fans who follow their chosen team through thick and thin. They are the real and genuine supporters who deserve great credit.

From the experience I have gained writing this book, I truly believe that if I can do it then anyone can – if they feel the need. If you have been thinking about it or delaying it because of a lack of confidence, it would give me a huge amount of satisfaction to know that someone did it after reading this. If that is the case, please let me know.

Finally, my words are dedicated to all of my family. I feel I have written this on their behalf. We are sharing with you the fun, laughter and the amazing times we have all been lucky enough to have experienced together during our lives. They are treasured times with much humour along the way – a certain person always guaranteed that – and I sincerely hope that you too can get to see the humorous side of things.

If your eyes can see through mine, then I know you will.

Enjoy the ride.

Saturday, March 28, 2015

During the season, Saturdays were always welcomed by Ben, especially after a busy weekly work schedule. Saturdays provided the chance to spend quality time with loved ones and his second family – team-mates at Stoke Gifford Football Club.

After the luxury of a little lie-in, it was business as usual at home, walking down the stairs holding the hand of little Aaliyah, the stepdaughter he idolised, heading to the kitchen to prepare breakfast.

But first there was the task of attending to Albert, the little dog they loved, which was done just before the arrival of Zoe, his future wife.

Around the breakfast table, plans were being finalised regarding the evening's entertainment, but Aaliyah was more interested in a promise Ben had made the evening before.

So then it was out with the eggs, flour and other ingredients for some lush cakes – a weekend treat. The cake-mixing bowl was the first to be cleaned, which involved rubbing fingers around the inside and then licking them. It was like a race they both loved and by the end the bowl would be spotless.

Later in the morning it was off to the local barber for a quick trim before returning to meet Zoe and Aaliyah at the local Co-op store. They were both going to the cinema in the afternoon so it was Ben's treat to buy them sweets to take with them.

Next stop was the home of a good friend, Barts. A few of the other lads were already there and the get-together had been planned because Bristol Rovers were live on TV in an early kick-off game. This allowed them to watch the first half before going off to Stoke Gifford for the afternoon game.

It was the biggest game of the season so far for the Gifford boys as the visitors were challenging for the title as well. All the lads noticed how Ben came over to them individually to encourage them and get their adrenaline going ahead of the game. As top goalscorer, a mantle he had held for many years, this top-of-the-table clash was one he desperately wanted to win, perhaps by adding to his tally of goals.

This became even more evident when he asked manager Martin Black if he could carry out the final team talk. Martin had previously played alongside Ben for a number of years. He explained: "The last few games we had not performed like I knew we could yet I couldn't pinpoint the reason why. Cox asked me and I certainly had no problem with it, so I left him to it."

Team-mate James Stephens said: "When Dennis (Ben) carried out the team talk it went silent. You could hear a pin drop. Everyone listened intently."

Ten minutes into the second half, Gifford were on the attack. Ben pulled out wide close to the touchline before receiving the ball. Having gone past one player, he was in full flight with the ball at his feet and a defender in hot pursuit. His aim was to get his cross into the goal area before the ball ran out of play. This meant he had to swing his right leg across his body, causing him to swing around 90 degrees or more in the process.

He struck the ball just as it reached the goal-line and at the same time received a nudge from a defender, which was enough to make his body rotate while he went flying through the air.

He then hit the ground and solid wall of the clubhouse at the same time, with the back of his head taking the full impact with a loud thud. He was left unconscious and his team-mates were shuddering over his safety. He was like that for five minutes or more. Two ambulance crews arrived, by which time he was sitting up on a chair but very agitated and restless, continually trying to rub the back of his head. It took a third medic to arrive and finally sedate him before he was rushed off to Southmead Hospital.

Suddenly, this Saturday was not so welcoming. This Saturday was now pivotal to Ben's life. This was a very cruel Saturday, the last he would ever grace the field at Stoke Gifford. Three days later, after suffering two seizures, 30-year-old Ben Hiscox died.

Chapter One

A STAR IS BORN

Born on November 28, 1956 I was the youngest of seven children and grew up in Lockleaze Road in Horfield, Bristol. Back then the longstanding joke in our numerous family was that mum and dad never had a telly! I always told my brothers and sisters they saved the best until last. They argued we might have been an even larger family until I came along – the risk of having another was just too much!

My earliest memories as a small child are of the beach at Weymouth. I loved the sea but hated the seaweed when it clung around my ankles. The seaweed was usually around the water's edge so I would always run into the sea as fast as I could to try and avoid it. Likewise when I came out.

It was a windy day and I was naked while my mum was drying me with a towel. A lady in front of me also had a towel around her and was smiling at me as we changed. Suddenly, there was a strong gust of wind and the lady's towel dropped down onto the sand. I was amazed but very concerned and immediately shouted: "Mum! That poor lady has some seaweed stuck to the top of her legs."

My mum hastily turned my head.

1

As a child I was certainly spoilt. My amateur dramatics also served me well in getting my own way. I was not a happy chappy when I didn't.

My eldest brother remembers spying on me. Apparently I was on the floor in the lounge, all alone, legs crossed, eating my tea from a plate on my lap while watching *Lassie* on TV. Whenever his owner told him to sit and stay, immediately his back was turned the dog would get up and follow him. In anger I instantly put my plate to one side, jumped up and ran over to the TV before shouting to Lassie: "Do as you are told – sit!" I could never understand why that dog did not listen to me.

Later, when I started infant school, I found the discipline very scary and was soon brought down to earth with a bump.

My earliest memories of comedy on TV – which captivated me and I loved to watch – are the many Marx Brothers films. They were old and made in black and white, but that didn't bother me. The eldest brother Groucho always seemed to have a cigar in his hand and moved around hastily, yet when he stopped in his tracks it was to come out with a classic one-liner that always made me laugh. The best, though, was the antics the two foolish younger brothers Chico and Harpo would always get up to. Harpo, especially, would leave me in stitches while I sat there, legs crossed, eyes glued on the TV until the end of the film.

As a youngster, Saturday was my favourite day by a million miles. It was the only day I was always up first in the morning – for a start, it was pocket money day – and then it was straight down to the local shop to purchase my weekly comic the *Tiger*, which featured Roy of the Rovers and many other of my heroes. I would keep sixpence (that's the small silver one) for later.

When the morning newspaper came through our letterbox, it didn't even hit the floor. I would grab it before checking out the afternoon's horse racing.

During the football season I always went off with my dad to play in the school game in the mornings, but in the afternoon it was down to some serious business. Me, my dad and brother Tony, who is 16 months older than me, would all write down our selections for the horse racing on TV. It was the ITV Seven hosted by Dickie Davies in which seven races were broadcast from different meetings.

My brother and I would put our sixpences into a tub and dad would put in a shilling, bringing the total to two shillings. This was big money. Three points were gained for picking a winner, two for second and one for third. If there was a close finish, I always stood up to ride out the race, slapping my own backside in an attempt to make my horse go faster

After the final race, the points tally was counted up. If I was lucky enough to have won, it was straight back down the shops. Oh yes! A large bottle of Tizer lemonade and a small bar of Wall's ice cream was enough to make a good few glasses of ice cream soda. Add to that a bar of white Nestlé chocolate – just like the Milky Bar Kid – and I was in heaven.

But if I did not win, boy was I a bad loser. I would sit around moping, wondering where it all went wrong. Playing in the background on the TV, I could hear motorcyclist Dave Bickers' name being continually mentioned, then wrestlers Steve Logan and Mick McManus. By the time Eddie Waring was commentating on the rugby league, I would be thinking about next Saturday and vowing to myself that I'd win.

Saturday evening was always a time to look forward to. My dad would nip off to our local Canton Chinese takeaway. On his return we would sit down and watch the football highlights while eating a lush curry – bliss ! What a day! Following that, I became one of the many who did not like Mondays!

I attended Filton Avenue Infant and Junior Schools before moving up to Lockleaze Secondary Modern School. During the four years at junior school, my most memorable yet embarrassing moment came in Year Two. In the mornings before going to our classrooms, we would all assemble in the main hall for service. In our school uniforms, we all sat on the floor with our legs crossed and arms folded with the eldest at the front and the younger classes at the rear.

On Fridays our headmaster Mr Chivers always mentioned where the school football team would be playing the following morning. He would then wish all the boys the best of luck. One particular Friday, everything seemed to be going as normal until the headmaster said that a piece of history was about to be made. To my astonishment he called out my name and asked me to stand up for everyone to see. Since I was nearer the back than the front, most heads had to swivel around to see who I was.

With my face the brightest red possible, the head said that I would be representing the school team for tomorrow's game and it was the first time ever that a second-year boy had gained a starting place. Following a round of applause, I was eventually allowed to sit back down.

Around that time one of my practical jokes backfired on me big time. My mum was waiting for a Mrs Tyler to visit and kept drumming in to me that I had to behave. I assumed the visitor was a good friend of my mum, so as she went to answer the door, I hid a whoopee cushion under one of the lounge chairs. Yes, the joke worked when Mrs Tyler sat on it. But she didn't see the funny side and I got sent to my bedroom. I later found out that Mrs Tyler had come to interview my mum for a part-time cleaning job. Oops!

A major regret from my younger days was losing track of my two scrapbooks. They took me ages to complete and today they would have been a treasure trove of memorabilia.

The books were devoted to every team in the Football League – with a page for each team. At the top was a team photo, and just below the club's official letter-headed paper with all the players' autographs on. Their nickname and home ground were next, leaving just enough room for some colour shots taken from the amazing *Charles Buchan's Football Monthly*, which was a big favourite of mine

I managed to get the autograph sheets by writing to each club claiming I was a lifelong supporter now living in Bristol. I said I rarely got the chance to see them play, but the clubs responded positively and sent me their letter-headed sheets.

Later, my writing skills improved even more and earned me some big money! I had quite a long letter about Bristol Rovers published in *Charles Buchan's Football Monthly*, saying the team were under-rated and mentioning a few of the Welsh internationals they had in the side at the time. I said I was confident they would soon be playing in Division One and later received £5 for my efforts. Bingo!

My boyhood hero was Jimmy Greaves. His skills and knack of scoring goals was amazing – like a magician. He swayed me towards supporting Spurs as my "other team".

I will never forget going to watch my very first game of professional football. It was in the early 1960s at Eastville Stadium in Bristol. My mum had knitted me a scarf and bobble hat to wear and I also had a rattle. I was amazed to see so many people wearing gear similar to me and everyone shook their rattles when the teams came out onto the pitch.

I remember a tall guy called Alfie Biggs scoring with a header and how the whole stadium erupted with joy. I fell in love with the blue and white quartered shirts the team were wearing and from that day my love affair with Bristol Rovers was born – and I was in it for life.

On the pitch as a youngster, I won a variety of trophies and medals at various levels but my playing days were cut short due to financial and personal reasons. But more of that later.

Love At First Sight

At junior school I was classified as mid-stream although, after knuckling down in the final year, I did manage to get up to the top stream when I attended Lockleaze Secondary. My dad was so impressed he offered me the chance to stay on and further my education at college or university.

But during the summer holidays, I got a part-time job at Tesco – and slowly but surely things started to change. Suddenly I had more money than ever before to spend on whatever I wanted. I wanted to leave school but after applying for a variety of jobs it soon became clear I was too young and would have to wait another year. My father insisted if I wanted to leave school I needed to learn a trade because "good tradesmen are never out of work".

So it was to be. I left school and went to work for a large engineering company called Drake and Scull on a four-year apprenticeship as a heating and plumbing engineer. I worked on a lot of different projects, commercial and domestic, and one day a week had to attend Brunel Technical College at Ashley Down in Bristol.

It was at college I met and gained a best mate – John Gibbs. What a character and true friend John turned out to be. We socialised together, played football for Lockleaze, went away on numerous holidays together and generally had so many good times. I even managed to convert John from his love of Led Zeppelin and rock music to the magical sounds of Motown and soul. Our friendship just grew stronger.

One morning, John rang me for a special favour. "Mate, I am at Eastville market with my sister and her kids. That bloody car of mine has given up the ghost on me again." John had a love-hate relationship with his Austin Cambridge. "Any chance of you popping down to give them a lift back home and then come back to tow this thing back to mine?"

So off I went down to the market. When I arrived John introduced me to his sister Gloria and her two sons Mark and Neil. My first reaction was to shake her hand but my thoughts were: "Wow! What an attractive lady." I joked with John about how someone as ugly as him could have such a beautiful sister. The more time I spent with Gloria it became obvious that she, like her brother, was a character in her own right. She oozed personality in abundance. In time, I could sense that her feelings were compatible with mine and the time we spent together became a time to cherish.

Our relationship grew stronger and stronger until we both decided we wanted to be together 24/7. So with Mark and Neil we both set up home in Toronto Road, Horfield, Bristol. As I was only starting the fourth year of my apprenticeship, money was very tight. My claim to fame in that era was that I'd actually started a trend – as Gloria was nearly 10 years older than me, I was the original toy boy!

We lived happily together for two years and 1978 was the happiest to date. We got married on May 27 and one of the proudest moments of my life happened on December 6 when Gloria gave birth to our daughter Rachel Elizabeth.

Within seconds of her arrival I held her blood-covered little body, which was wrapped in a towel. I vowed to love and keep her safe forever. We had happy times until four years later, life dealt us our first real blow – and a cruel one. On September 4, 1982 Gloria was about to give birth to our second child at Southmead Hospital. Excitement and anticipation were at their maximum but sadly our second daughter Zoe was stillborn

No words could explain my grief. On my own, I attended her burial at Bedminster Down, South Bristol. This was easily the saddest day in my life so far. Should we now count our blessings and be grateful for the children we already have between us, or should we try just one more time before accepting that our family is then complete?

Chapter Two

ANOTHER STAR IS BORN

After careful consideration and advice from the medical staff, we both agreed to try one more time. So when Gloria did announce she was pregnant, our feelings this time were excitement and nervousness.

We were advised it would be for the best if the birth was carried out by Caesarean section, which we both agreed to. On June 20, 1984 things were starting to happen so later that day, after a couple of phone calls, we were advised to come into Southmead Hospital to prepare for the birth.

Shortly after settling into the ward, we were on the move. I helped push Gloria's bed as we headed towards the theatre. Just before entering I was taken to one side and shown into another room. It was a small changing room with lots of surgical clothes on hangers. I had to change before going into theatre. By now it was approaching 7pm, very humid and I could feel my body temperature rising fast as it was the most worrying and nervous time of my life. Suddenly the door burst open and in rushed a guy who barely looked at me before hastily changing into similar attire as me. "Just my bloody luck!" he said. Let's hope this is done and dusted quickly. I'm going to a party. Five more minutes and I would have been gone. Damn!"

With that the guy stopped and looked over at me. He could see that I was nervous and confused. I mumbled that I needed to be with my wife because I was the father. I could sense that he was embarrassed by what he'd said, but to be fair he put an arm around my shoulder, told me not to worry and that everything was going to be fine. With that, he led me into the theatre.

Thankfully, everything went to plan. It was a magical moment when our little boy came into the world. He was very carefully lifted to a height where his proud mum could get a glimpse of her newborn son. Without hesitation, he promptly emptied his bladder. The medical staff and I were all amazed at the distance he managed to get while spraying his mum's face. What a shot! Welcome to the world, Ben Clive Hiscox.

I still remember laughing and crying at the same time – something I'd become accustomed to. At night, I had always dealt with the nappy-changing and bottle-feeding regime with Rachel. Now it was only right this little lad received the same service.

Ben's arrival, however, did present us with a little problem. Our house at Toronto Road was a three-bed semi and we now really needed something bigger. It was a case of either moving or extending, and since I was involved in the building industry we opted for the latter. Although it took 16 months, we eventually completed a ground and first-floor extension providing a ground-floor loo, dining and office rooms as well as providing a first-floor bathroom and two additional bedrooms. For our youngest, our house was now looking much more like a home.

Once Ben started crawling, like most babies that age, he was always very curious and adventurous. Yet even at that age, and with all the toys he had available, the biggest attraction was always crawling towards his smiley rubber ball. He'd throw it one-handed, then watch it bounce before crawling along to repeat the whole exercise again. I must admit I did encourage him along the way. We even had crawling races to see who could get to the ball first – although I usually let him win.

After saving money for quite a while, we managed to buy our first Betamax video recorder. Gloria's favourite comedy act was Cannon and Ball so this enabled her to record the complete TV series, plus a full-length film shown on TV called *The Boys In Blue*. Usually Ben was not that bothered about TV yet he found Bobby Ball quite fascinating. In time, he got captivated by the TV series and the film, probably because his mum watched them so often. It got to a stage where he would sit in front of the TV and not move when it was on, often eating his meals from a plate on his lap during episodes.

When we arrived in Weymouth to stay in a lovely, cosy flat for our summer holiday, Ben got quite upset in the evening when we flicked on the TV to see what was on. He kept crying out: "Ball! Ball!" hoping we could put his favourite programme on. Consequently, we ended up listening to the radio until he went to bed. Needless to say that on our return home, his wishes were granted and he could play catch-up with the series while we unpacked the cases.

Bed times with Ben – and his toys – were a ritual. He had six little mates to sleep with – Eddie the elephant, Donald the duck, Pat the potato head, Guy the gorilla, Roger the rabbit, and Ted the teddy bear. I would put on a different voice for each of them, although this had to be maintained to perfection or he would look at me suspiciously. Each one would tell him all about their day and what they'd been up to before asking him likewise. Finally, they all kissed him before wishing him "Niber niber!" See you in the morning!

Ben soon started to form a close relationship with his sister Rachel, who not only played with him and protected him but showed lots of patience when they spent time together. Her love for him was plain to see. The two were inseparable when watching a certain programme on TV – both very wary of *The Incredible Hulk*. Together they hugged and hid behind the settee when his size increased, only coming back out when his size returned to normal.

Another programme that scared the hell out of Ben was *Worzel Gummidge*. He couldn't resist watching it and everything was fine until Worzel's head turned around full circle. Like a flash, he was gone.

However, he did have a clear second favourite to Bobby Ball. When *Postman Pat* (and his black and white cat) came on, he always stood up and danced to the theme tune – both at the start and the end.

All Change

Ben attended his first playgroup at St Gregory's Church in Horfield - his first chance to mingle with other toddlers his age. At first he looked around at everyone a little cautiously, but the more his little playmates approached him, the more he gained confidence. Soon he was off leading the way while being followed by smiling little faces.

One sunny summer day, Gloria, Rachel and Ben were out in the garden enjoying the fresh air. It was a large garden with plenty of play space, but it did require a lot of maintenance. However, this particular day was going to be life-changing for us all.

Gloria was hanging out the washing and Rachel had popped back into the house. After hanging out the last item of washing, Gloria turned around to check on Ben - but he was nowhere to be seen. After calling to Rachel and checking inside the house, alarm bells started to ring. Panic stricken, she started calling out his name as she raced up and down the road, but there was still no sign of him. Knowing this was quite a busy road, things were becoming desperate. The minutes seemed like hours and there was still no sign of him.

Then, suddenly, Gloria heard a voice. It was our neighbour Mr Marchant calling from his garden. "We seem to have a visitor," he said. Gloria and Rachel raced around to see Ben in the garden. Gloria felt like giving Mr Marchant an enormous kiss, but thanked him profusely and took Ben back home.

For our part, the most concerning thing was that the only possible way Ben could have escaped was through the hedge, which runs parallel to Toronto Road. Thankfully, he must have walked down the kerb side before turning left into Hazel Grove and Mr Marchant's garden. He did this not by the gate, which was closed, but through his hedge as well.

When I returned home from work, I was made aware of what had happened and we sat down to share our thoughts. Our minds were clearly made up. The house was put straight on the market and we were looking to move sooner rather than later.

Chapter Three

ALL CHANGE TAKE TWO

For various reasons we wanted a low-maintenance house which met most, if not all, of our requirements. A relatively new one would be ideal. We were fortunate with our sale, which enabled us to buy a four-bedroom house in Little Stoke, Bristol. It had been recently built by Bryant Homes. We were all excited and looking forward to moving in.

The garden had one side of panelled fencing, which was good. The other had small concrete posts with thin wire stretching between them. This was not so good, especially with Ben being Ben, and would have to be our first modification.

Our neighbours on the other side of the wire fence were two ladies, who at first seemed to be welcoming yet shortly after did not seem to take kindly to us.

Ben started to go to playgroup at Little Stoke Baptist Church and became popular with the other toddlers, as well as the mums. The impact his personality had on them – with his short, spikey hair and toothless, cheeky grin – was soon noticed and remarked upon by the other smiling mums.

Another ritual around this time was the *Sooty and Sweep* puppet show. Ben would always sit down with me and watch the puppets carrying out some interesting monologues. He got seriously involved when my head was turned away and the puppets got up to no good without me knowing. He got even louder when I returned my head to the previous position, asking what had gone on – especially after both puppets had pleaded innocent to any wrongdoing. He would then assure me in no uncertain terms that they had! In the background, Rachel was often cracking up at the antics. I sometimes had to cut short the performance for public health reasons.

Our stay at Silverbirch Close was unfortunately cut short. Firstly, attempts to replace the wire fencing with more substantial wood panelling were not greeted too well by our neighbours. During the works an empty cement bag accidentally flew into their garden. One of the women angrily returned it to us and, even in front of the children, let rip with a tirade of foul language, some of which even I had never heard.

The following week one of my business suppliers pulled up outside in a small van with a few items I had ordered. In an attempt not to restrict other traffic, he temporarily parked across a small part of our neighbours' drive before swiftly running over to our front door with the items.

On his return to his van, he was spoken to by one of the women. After the dialogue, the driver quickly pulled away before parking up around the corner and returning to knock on my door. He said in all the years he had been delivering he had never been spoken to like that before. He drove off not a happy man.

The final straw came with a letter from the council which said it had received a complaint. I would now need a licence to park my own signed van on my own driveway. My rates would increase if I was running a business from my own home. I must ensure staff did not park their vehicles across driveways. The letter went on with more ridiculous things I should abide by.

I felt very angry. I was quite prepared to fight for our rights but the reality was that my wife had been distraught and very unhappy. It had affected her badly. She could not relax in her own home and, when going out, always had to keep looking over her shoulder. Talks were short this time and up went the For Sale sign again. At least our local estate agent was smiling.

This time I was determined to ensure that our new home was in a location that was peaceful, friendly and ticked all the boxes we needed. We checked out the lovely village of Stoke Gifford. And in fact we ended up just a stone's throw away. They had only recently started building Bradley Stoke and Robbins \close was just the other side of the dual carriageway from Gifford. Surely this was the right place for us? It certainly did tick all the boxes.

Ben celebrated his fourth birthday not long after we moved in. We had already checked out that Little Stoke infant and junior schools were close at hand, as was Filton High senior school. Now we were smiling again and really could look forward to the future. Little Stoke playing fields were also close at hand, a place we would soon get to know very well.

Having already studied at university in Nottingham for a while, Mark decided he wanted to live there, which meant we'd see a lot less of him.

One of my first jobs after moving in was to make a safe and secure play area for Ben. With such a large garden at the back I decided to replace a large part of it and build a large patio area ideal for bike riding or kicking a ball, which he loved.

Our first nickname for Ben came from when we were out driving. He often tried to look around to take in the scenery, but it was quite difficult for him because of his size and the restriction of the seat belt, which meant he really had to stretch his head as high up as possible to see out of the window. At times it appeared as though his head was about to part company with his shoulders, which would then produce a quiet whisper: "I think Ben's doing his impression of ET again."

Summer and Seasonal Cheer

Christmas was always a very exciting time at home. Well after bedtime, you could hear Rachel and Ben talking in their bedroom, laughing and having fun – especially in the lead-up to Christmas. Thankfully, Rachel's sweet talk provided a calming influence which usually got him off to sleep.

Christmas morning had a familiar pattern for a few years. In the all-too-early hours of the morning, we'd congregate on the landing. Then the main question would be asked: Had Santa been? There was only one way to find out, so we'd all tiptoe down the stairs before lining up outside the lounge door. The rules were to line up in single file, youngest at the front and eldest at the rear (poor mum!). The youngest would then slowly and quietly open the door – just in case Santa was still in the room. Ben, to be fair, played his part to the hilt. But once that door was fully open he was like a whippet – gone!

Rachel was always close behind. The silence was broken with cheers of delight and the sheer joy and excitement on their faces made it all worthwhile.

Another nice thing about our new home was the hallway, which provided us with an excellent football pitch on the evenings when the others were in the lounge doing their own thing. There is a seven-metre space between the front door and the kitchen entrance door. Both doors became goalmouths for us to defend. We played with a soft ball and you could only shoot at the opposition goal from inside your own half. Passing the halfway line was offside.

Ben and I would dress in full kit – unsurprisingly either Bristol Rovers or Tottenham. When one person had scored five goals it was half time and we changed ends. The first person to 10 was the winner.

Ben always had the first choice of which team he was going to represent, regardless of the kit we were wearing. We both often chose various teams and although I won the odd game, it was only when I represented Rovers or Tottenham so Ben would usually end up winning. I always provided an excited commentary all the way through, right to the final whistle. We played hundreds of games over the years yet there was one thing even Ben never picked up on. How come neither Bristol Rovers nor Tottenham ever lost – or got to play against each other?

All my efforts building the patio seemed to be in vain. Robbins Close is a quiet cul-de-sac so Ben would often be out the front on the tarmac road kicking a ball about, which was generally safe. If I'm honest, I'd often join him and we spent hours doing what we both enjoyed.

Even at a young age, Ben always mixed well with other toddlers –either at playgroup or at home – so it was no surprise when he befriended Ryan and Damian Bickford. They were sons of our new neighbours Shirley and Martin.

Together they became inseparable, playing games as youngsters do. Lunch or snacks were usually eaten together at either of the two homes. In fact, it was down to these young guys that Robbins Close became a safer place to live.

All three were into the *Teenage Mutant Ninja Turtles*. Ben used to love putting on the outfit of his favourite Michelangelo, while Ryan and Damian dressed as Raphael and Donatello. Together they roamed around the close keeping it a villain-free area.

The four of us started to visit Twerton Park in Bath on match days to watch Bristol Rovers. Gerry Francis was the manager and the young ones soon had their own favourite players. Maybe it was because we stood behind the goal but Rachel soon developed a liking for goalkeeper Nigel Martyn. Ben, on the other hand, had two favourites - little midfielder Ian Holloway and big striker Devon White.

They soon both became quite vocal during the games, which they really seemed to enjoy – and the half-time attraction of a Cornish pasty was always very welcome.

Ben was excited although a little nervous about starting at Little Stoke Infants. He made a few visits in preparation before term commenced. He got to meet his new teacher Mrs Callow each time he visited, which saw his confidence grow thanks to her friendly manner and attitude towards him.

Summer breaks were becoming more enjoyable than ever. We always headed to the south coast where we stayed on a campsite, either in a chalet or caravan. Our days often began with myself, Rachel and Ben rising early but quietly before driving off to the harbour, where we all got to drop our lines in the sea for a spot of crabbing. There was always a prize for the one who caught the most. Our catch was kept in a water-filled bucket and the crabs were always returned to the sea when we left.

Before that though was inspection time and between us we could recognise by size and colour exactly who caught each individual crab. It was strange how after catching a few, my quota always seemed to be nil.

After heading back for breakfast, we would all then go off to the beach. Barely before we'd had time to put up the deckchairs and windbreak, Ben would slip into his trunks and be off for a quick dip in the sea. Meanwhile, in the sand, I'd mark out a tennis court, followed by a cricket pitch, not forgetting the goalmouth for football, of course, or a hole in the sand ready for a game of golf.

All the while, Gloria would be soaking up the sun – weather permitting. Bless!

We'd usually return to the campsite just in time for tea before ending the day in the clubhouse with some well-earned and much-needed liquid refreshments.

Since the boys' *Ninja Turtles* outfits had been cast aside, Robbins Close had obviously become a more vulnerable place and residents were getting quite concerned. All that suddenly changed one gloomy, foggy day when out of the mist appeared a young boy wearing dungaree overalls complete with a back-pack. He was holding a lightning ray gun in one hand and a ghost trap in the other. Who ya gonna call? It was Ben. He was a ghostbuster of course. Soon his two mates joined him wearing their outfits and once again they patrolled the close, keeping us all safe again. We all owed a huge debt to these guys and once again we could sleep with total peace of mind.

Once Ben started infant school, he soon increased his circle of friends in his reception class at Little Stoke. His crew-cut hairstyle and cheeky grin increased his popularity significantly. At the school gates, other parents spoke kindly of him and made us well aware how friendly he had become with their own children. Most of them said he had become their best friend, something we were destined to hear more of.

His popularity meant numerous little faces would appear at our front door after school, accompanied by a parent. They had come to play and have fun with Ben, often staying for tea before Gloria or I took them back home later.

However, there was one occasion when Ben was not so happy. His friend Chris Church recalls: "My very first memory of Ben has to be when his mum Gloria didn't arrive at school on time to pick him up. I lived fairly close to school so once I was old enough I was able to walk there and back. Ben lived a little further away so he was picked up and dropped off.

"On this one occasion he was stood on his own looking tearful and a bit lost. I waited alongside him until Gloria arrived. As soon as he saw his mum, the tears stopped and his smile returned."

And a true friendship had just begun.

The games being played in our close were becoming more popular, especially when I was around to kick a ball – which seemed to encourage some of the older lads. In fact, many youngsters started coming along to enjoy our games of football – although, unfortunately, one of the older neighbours did not take too kindly to it.

The front gardens to most of the houses are small and open, most with paths leading up to the front door. One day one of the boys went to retrieve the ball from our neighbour's path but was greeted with some harsh words and told to go and play elsewhere. Even when I sneakily tried to tip-toe along her path to pick up the ball, I was caught red handed and given a severe ticking off – a future format was soon to follow which would carry on for many years!

Chapter Four

NEW TEAM, NEW MANAGER

The football season was coming to a nail-biting finish for Bristol Rovers. Our neighbours Bristol City were two points ahead of us at the top of the table with two games left. The penultimate one, an evening kick-off at Twerton Park, was against none other than our deadly rivals.

Because of the kick-off time, the two young ones were unable to go – which they weren't happy about, having seen most of the other home games. But we did allow them to stay up and listen to the commentary on BBC Radio Bristol. We all sat and listened to a very close game until Devon White scored. We clapped and cheered excitedly, but I said we should all remain calm as there was still a long way to go. All that went out of the window when Ian Holloway scored from a penalty late in the game. We all rose up, dancing around the room, hugging and kissing each other, waving our hands in the air as if we'd just won the World Cup! It's fair to say we were delighted.

To complete the season, Rovers won 3-0 at Blackpool to finish as champions. We were on the up!

Italia 90 was the first World Cup that Ben became aware of. He watched the England games and many of the others very closely and got very excited at the quarter-final stage watching a rollercoaster game between England and Cameroon, with Gary Lineker scoring a winning penalty in extra time. Following that came the agony of losing out yet again to arch-rivals Germany on penalties.

Ben's favourite player was Paul Gascoigne – Gazza – who performed admirably throughout the competition. I can still recall Ben looking sad and concerned when Gazza was shown on TV proudly holding the badge of his England shirt while crying in the Germany game.

Our summer vacation that year took us to Norton Park holiday camp near Dartmouth in Devon. We had active days with the new addition of kite-flying on a local beach. We never really mastered the art and I had to keep swimming out to sea to rescue our fallen one. Bigbury-on-Sea also provided us with beach games when the tide was out, and Bantham Beach gave us our first taste of surfing, which we all really enjoyed.

Back at the camp we often took part in the games and competitions in the evening. Rachel won the talent contest singing a song called *Crazy*, which was originally sung by Patsy Cline. I decided to get involved in the karaoke competition and ended up winning, singing Gene Pitney's *Something's Gotten Hold Of My Heart*. Ben needed a huge amount of persuasion to take part in the fancy dress competition. We had all the costume for him to be a pirate, but he was very reluctant. As luck would have it, because Bristol Rovers' nickname is the Pirates, we convinced him he would be representing our club – and our tactic worked! He entered and duly won. On our final evening, Gloria won a full house on the bingo so she was in the money. We all came away happy having had a good time.

As Little Stoke playing fields were only a couple of minutes away, I got into the habit of getting home from work as soon as I could. This enabled me to pop Ben into my van – complete with kit and boots – before going for a kickabout. Little did we know just how popular our visits would eventually become.

At first a few lads a bit older than Ben asked if they could join in our game. I welcomed them so between us we made up two teams and played several games, with the first team to score five goals winning. We then swapped the teams around and started again. Soon, lots of young lads of various ages started turning up wanting to join our games and word started to spread. Before long, youngsters from Stoke Gifford, Stoke Lodge, Patchway and Filton were coming along to enjoy the fun.

New lads would come along and introduce themselves before I told them the rules they would have to abide by. I appointed two captains and as the age levels varied, if a captain chose an older lad to play in his team then he had to have a younger one as his next pick, and vice versa. This gave both teams a mixed age range, which was fair. The older boys were not allowed to make full-strength tackles on the younger ones. As for me, I always ended up playing for the team I thought were underdogs – and since I also refereed all the games, my decision was final.

We never played our games on the marked out pitches at the park – it was always at the far bottom end using jumpers or tops for goalposts. After a while, a typical evening would see all the lads sitting down on the grass or milling around talking to each other as they waited for us to arrive. As soon as I pulled into the car park with Ben, they would all run over to greet us with nice smiles and comments. It was a lovely welcome.

During the Christmas holiday period, another pattern was formed which was to last for a few years. Our home became the venue for all of our family to come and socialise on Boxing Night.

To get things going, Gloria and I would put on a bit of a show for our guests – we would dress up, sing, dance and generally make fools of ourselves – yet we all loved it. Rachel usually sang – with or without her cousin – and when she did the room fell silent because of her amazing voice, which always guaranteed the loudest applause of the evening.

Ben, meanwhile, was in the process of learning to do what he did best. Along with cousins Lloyd and Gavin, they rehearsed their act up in his bedroom before coming down to the lounge. Then, to our delight, they performed a montage of comical sketches, jokes, one-liners and even the odd impersonation. They bounced off each other in a hilarious way. These performances certainly encouraged Ben to play act as well as use his own wit to create laughter all around – certainly something he seemed to enjoy.

We all sang, ate and drank plenty as the night went on. I always organised some adults versus children games, which were very competitive as well as great fun. Needless to say, the youngsters always won – but we never made it too easy for them. This was our Christmas – the time of year we all got together to enjoy each other's company with love and affection.

The other seasonal venue for a get-together was just across the road in Stoke Gifford. It was the home of my brother Tony who – along with his wife Tina and children Lloyd, Gavin, Dawn and Faye – provided our New Year's Eve celebrations. We carried on the fun in much the same fashion before welcoming in the new year. As a group we all went outside to form a huge circle, crossing our arms and linking together to sing *Auld Lang Syne*. We did it in our own way – but a way that was never forgotten.

An Exceptional Talent

Eastville was popular for its market days but it also provided another attraction – greyhound racing. So one Saturday evening I decided to take Rachel and Ben along with me and have a little flutter on each race. In a determined mood and looking to prove my gambling skills, I bought a programme which gave lots of information about every dog in each race. I studied it in great depth before making my selections. In between consuming popcorn, lemonade and crisps, the young ones casually made theirs.

For some reason Ben would always choose dog number two. By contrast, Rachel studied the dogs and would make her choice based on its colour, size or even its cuteness – whichever she thought the most relevant. We all cheered our dogs as they ran around the track but by the end of the evening I had not had one winner – yet both the youngsters were quids in, lucky devils! On our way home it suddenly dawned on me why Ben always went for dog number two – it always had a blue jacket. Should have known really!

As the spring arrived, cricket was also becoming popular with Ben. At the rear of the house three wickets were marked on a wall ready for play. We often took a stroll down to the nets at our local Baileys Court cricket club and took it in turns to bat and bowl. Ben's batting was quite good and his bowling very good. We also started to pay a few visits to the County Ground to watch Gloucestershire play. It made an enjoyable day with our packed lunches keeping us going.

During the school summer holidays, word had had got around from some of Ben's older friends that our local Stoke Lane Athletic Youth Football Club were advertising for youngsters to come along to training sessions, held on Saturday mornings at Little Stoke playing fields. Ben was keen to go along as some of his older friends were already playing for Stoke Lane. I was curious to see how the club worked with the youngsters as it had a growing reputation at youth level.

The following Saturday we went along to the park and were welcomed by the manager, as were many other parents. We then watched the training and talked among ourselves. Ben was easy to pick out as he was the smallest of the group – I later found out that some were a year or two older. At the end of the session the manager talked to the boys before speaking with parents individually. He made it clear he thought Ben looked an exciting prospect. He was a little concerned about his size and age – Ben was one of youngest in his year at school. He then asked if I could bring him back the following week, which I was happy to do.

In fact, we returned the following four Saturdays. I was so pleased to see how Ben was improving each week. OK, most of the other boys were bigger and more physical in strength, but the natural talent and ability that he had was blatantly obvious. I was now feeling optimistic that he could be part of a recognised team and that I could go and watch him weekly throughout the season. Things were looking good.

Back home, Neil had occasionally been living with a friend and it was no surprise when he made the decision that he wanted to house share with him permanently, so we all helped him make the move.

This presented us with the opportunity to make big changes at home with two bedrooms ready to be completely stripped and redecorated. A sporting theme was the idea for one, with bright colours and lots of wardrobe space for the other. For the youngsters this meant the first chance since Toronto Road to have their own bedrooms – and this was especially welcomed by the elder of the two. In time, the skip outside would be full to capacity.

The fifth and final Saturday morning of football training came about and it was back down to the park with the rest of the Stoke Lane boys. We were both eager and excited, only to be hit by a bombshell.

After training the manager gathered all the boys around him – there were about 22 in all. He then pointed to 16 of the lads and asked if they would go over to the goalmouth area and wait for him there. He then told the remaining six – including Ben – that unfortunately they would not be part of the squad for the coming season.

Ben slowly walked away looking down at the ground and was very disappointed. I put my arm on his shoulder and walked with him to the car. As I drove away, I felt both angry and cheated. I did not know how this could happen after witnessing training over the previous five weeks. It was just not right. My thoughts deepened and I worried that the decision could affect Ben's confidence. He did not deserve this.

Back at the house, I told Gloria I was going back to the playing fields alone to have a word with the manager. As I pulled up, I could see some of the other parents in the same situation as me already talking to him. Most of them had begun to disperse as I walked over. I spoke with the manager for quite a while. He was very apologetic and explained that regarding Ben's case in particular, he could be playing against some boys nearly two years older and at his young age that could hamper his natural progress. I could see a valid point in his reasoning, but what he then proposed gave me massive food for thought.

Due to the nature of my work at this time, I had to leave home very early and quietly in the morning. But when pulling away from our drive, I did often notice the curtain in the upstairs window move slightly and a small, smiling face appear as Ben waved me off. I always returned the smile and wave before leaving.

During my conversation with the manager, I noticed that the other parents had congregated in the distance and were still talking amongst themselves.

The manager then asked me if I would consider managing, training and generally organising an Under-8 Stoke Lane football team. He explained that he would be taking this bunch of boys into the Hanham Minor League at Under-9 level, which was the youngest recognised age level for youngsters in youth football at that time. He explained that although there was no official Under-8 league, many other local youth teams were playing friendlies in an effort to help prepare and provide experience for their boys. They would then likewise enter the Hanham Minor League the next season.

He then said that even next season Ben would be one of the youngest in the team — that is, if I was prepared to take it on. I would be given contact numbers for the other managers and we would arrange friendly games, gradually building up a fixture list for the season ahead. I would be provided with kit, the use of pitches and changing rooms at Little Stoke, as well as midweek training facilities. In return, I would have to take full responsibility for forming a squad, carrying out training, attending meetings, collecting and paying out money to cover fees…the list of duties went on and on. But in fact, the longer it got the more my mind was made up. Eventually my eagerness got the better of me. "OK mate, no problem. Yes, I'll do it!"

As I said the words, my thoughts changed. Here I am, accepting a time-consuming role, without even consulting my wife. Oops, what have I done?

As our meeting concluded, the other parents came over to learn about our discussions and were really happy when I invited their lads to be part of my squad. Gary Monks, with his son Sean, was among the parents and offered to help me in any way he could, which I was very grateful for.

But my search was now on for another dozen or so lads to play football. Before that, I also had to attend a number of meetings at Stoke Lane. But before any or even all of that, I had the small issue of telling Gloria about my decision.

Ben seemed to be really enjoying school, especially with so many friends around him. When we were not at the fields, one or two always came back home with him after school. It soon became apparent that they all shared the same interests. They all had a genuine love for sport, which is why a ball was usually involved in all of their games.

Luckily for me, Gloria backed my decision. She made it clear that she was well aware of Ben's capabilities and love of the game. Not only was she happy with it, her involvement and help would be huge in the time to come.

At the meetings, I was supplied with a vast amount of information and contact numbers. Suddenly the amount of names and numbers in my phone book quadrupled.

Having approached other local schools to make them aware – along with Ben's friends at Little Stoke – my squad of boys slowly started to increase ahead of our first game.

Chris Church says: "Ben was a very good footballer who had started at an early age. However, I was a late starter. My football career kicked off when Ben invited me to join him at a Stoke Lane training session. I loved it and continued to train and play. Looking back, I'm really thankful that he invited me along."

Chapter Five

THE AWARDS BEGIN

Excitement was building with our very first friendly game just around the corner – although the saying "there's a lot of work to be done" was very fitting afterwards. We lost 16-0. But thanks to their young age, the result did not appear to affect the confidence of the boys, who played wearing kit that was far too big – though they all loved it.

Although we lost our next six pre-arranged games, the scorelines were becoming more respectable. And after a trip to Nailsea, things started to change. We came in at the interval three goals down but then went out for the second half and gave as good as we got. Ben scored a hat-trick and we ended up drawing 3-3. We still have the boots he wore that day. It was so good to see all the boys embracing and smiling together.

The next game was a landmark for us. We travelled just up the road to play Frampton Cotterell and Ben scored the only goal of the game. Somehow the rest of the boys managed to pick Ben up and carry him off the pitch to the changing room, which became a buzzing place full of happy, smiling faces.

We ended our friendly campaign with two more victories. Now we were preparing for life at Under-9 level in the Hanham Minor League.

The prospect of redecorating the first of the two bedrooms had Ben and I excited. The main wall, which catches the eye as soon as you enter, became a combination of blue and white to honour our favourite team. The wall opposite was divided into two with the top half white and the bottom dark navy to honour our second team. Stoke Lane played in black and white stripes so we incorporated this as a border design. Gloria, however, insisted that the window wall be wallpapered, so a compromise was agreed – especially as it was out of view when the curtains were fully drawn. Ha ha!

During the summer we bought a touring caravan to accommodate my business needs, which were proving to be very time consuming. This allowed us to pop off down south to holiday camps either for long weekends or short breaks at short notice. This helped provide me with quality time with my family away from the demands of my business.

Our destination was Hoburne Park at Christchurch, near Bournemouth. We were looking to join in with the fun weekend of games and activities on offer. Lots of other families clearly had the same idea as the park was pretty full when we got there. But we managed to set up base before buying a programme with all the details of the weekend's events.

On Saturday at 10am a five-a-side football competition began, played on grass, with teams of all ages and sizes taking part. Rachel and Ben were both excited but Gloria felt she would rather watch than play, so I managed to find two teenage boys who were looking to take part and happy to become part of the Hiscox team. We won two games to make it through to the semi-finals.

Rachel was our goalkeeper, I played in defence, the two teenagers were in midfield and we had Ben as our only striker. Our tactics were proving to be very successful. Ben tended to remain up the pitch while I stayed back to hold the fort and the energetic teenage lads chased, hustled and bustled and generally made a nuisance of themselves to win the ball. Because Ben was so small the opposition tended to leave him alone, thinking he was no danger. More fool them.

Most times when we managed to get the ball up to him he would not only control it well but keep it at his feet. His dribbling skills were excellent – as was his deadly finishing. He soon became our top scorer.

At the semi-final stage, a crowd was beginning to form around the pitch and things were starting to get a bit more serious. I was one of the four members of our team starting to get a bit nervous. Only one appeared to be cool, calm and collected and that was Ben, who could not wait to get out on the pitch and play.

Our opponents were from Oxford and they went 1-0 up, but luckily for us they had not done their homework on our tactics. Just before half-time, we got the ball up to Ben who scored an equaliser. The crowd roared and applauded loudly, probably because of Ben's size and our tag as the underdogs.

The game was tight until late on when I managed to win the ball and – probably thanks to the four Shredded Wheat I had eaten earlier – managed to go on a run towards goal. Although a couple of defenders forced me out wide, I was still able to force the ball towards their goalmouth. No prizes for guessing who was waiting there to calmly control the ball before tucking it away. The crowd applauded even louder – everyone seemed to want us to win. Ben soaked up all the post-match plaudits with his typical cheeky smile.

As the final began, it became clear our opponents, who were from Hastings in Sussex, had done their homework. Ben was now being man marked by a guy aged around 40. This actually did us a favour as it gave the rest of us more space to exploit. In fact, one of the lads took full advantage of this just before half-time and gave us a 1-0 lead.

During the second half, though, we were starting to tire and the crowd erupted when Rachel pulled off an absolutely amazing save. I never knew she had that in her locker!

Full credit to Ben, especially as the service to him was now non-existent. He still managed to get himself around the pitch tirelessly, often coming back to help out in defence. Our opponents paid him great respect by never letting him out of their sights. We finally made it to the final whistle and I will never forget the sight of everyone cheering as they ran on. No prizes again for guessing who got most pats on the back and was top goalscorer of the competition.

During the evening, there was a presentation and it was so nice and respectful when we went up on stage to receive our medals. Ben got the biggest cheer of the night by cheekily kissing his.

We took part in many other games and activities over the weekend and met and gained many new friends, particularly in the evenings when we socialised in the main clubroom. Rachel and Ben mixed well with other youngsters too, making new friends – which was good to see. And it came in between frequent visits to the arcade, where Rachel would be checking out the latest video games while Ben would be deciding which fruit machine to chance his arm on. We all came away with big smiles and looking forward to a return visit.

On TV, the cricket World Cup was being shown from Australia and Ben followed England's performances with much excitement as they made it through to the final, only to lose out narrowly to Pakistan.

At home, bedroom two was being redecorated with a much brighter and more colourful design, which the two ladies were both insisting on. A new era was about to happen in the English Football League. Division One was being replaced and along with other top teams, Tottenham would be playing in the new Premier League.

Just before we played our first game in the Hanham Minor League as Stoke Lane Under-9s, I started and continued writing two books, which I still have. These cover every single game we ever played under my official management (not including Under-8s) and start on September 6, 1992 and end on April 25, 1999.

In both books it shows the date at the top of each page along with our opponents. Just below that is the team I selected plus the substitutes, with a tick if they got to play. After this I wrote the scoreline and goalscorers with the bottom half of the page left for a description of how the game unfolded and how the players expressed themselves. These pages helped to keep an up-to-date, consistent and fair analysis of their efforts, enabling me to make the tough decisions needed when I picked the team each week.

I did not believe in a rotation system but it was important that all the lads had a fair crack of the whip, so after each game I would sit quietly at home to write up the details while they were still fresh in my mind. It became a habit I stuck to.

Gloria was my unsung hero and what a help she proved to be. She took complete control of the team finances, collecting and keeping record of all subscriptions – not just for games and training, but pre-arranged fun days, summer tours, Christmas or end-of-season parties and much more. She provided our half-time oranges plus little treats to the lucky lad who won man of the match or gained the exceptional effort awards after each game. She was very much part of the team.

Back down at the playing fields our games of football were becoming even more popular and quite intense with all the lads playing to win. Scorewise it was always very close but I must give huge credit to all the lads, especially the older ones, for the way they conducted themselves and accepted all my decisions gracefully.

Although Ben was one of the youngest, he always held his own throughout the games and the experience he gained without doubt helped him to improve his game as a player and team member.

|I gained a lot of satisfaction when the two nominated captains would pick their teams because Ben would always be the first pick of the younger lads.

Two of the lads who played regularly have written their own version of events at the playing fields. Tim Walsh, a journalist and sports reporter for ITV, wrote: "It was always a treat to see Clive and Ben pull up in the car park. Ben must have been only six or seven back then. He'd come running over with a big smile and excitedly tell us how he'd scored a great goal at school that day.

"We had some great games. So many people turned up – not just those who lived nearby but from further afield too. There would regularly be 15-20 people, the youngest Ben's age and the oldest 16 or 17. The younger guys knew they could take on the older ones without the risk of an over-physical challenge.

"Even at that age, Ben was a good footballer. He scored a lot of goals each night. Playing with older kids probably helped his development.

"Clive acted as referee and was very fair. There were people of all abilities and everyone got on with each other. It was like one big, happy family. If I am honest, they were the happiest times of my life.

"Sometimes you would get kids joining in who no-one knew. They were just passing and wondered why there were so many people playing football when it wasn't an organised event. They would join in and soon be part of the family – and the next night they'd be back with some of their friends. It just grew and grew."

Another regular at the fields Stuart Ellison, who works in banking with NatWest, recalled: "I will always remember the first time I saw Clive and Ben turn up at the fields. They were in a long wheelbase, high-top, garish yellow Transit van which would become a symbol of many of our childhood evenings.

"The first time they emerged from the van it was apparent they were like two peas in a pod. Both had huge smiles and the same cheeky grin, and both had an infectious sense of humour.

"Even after the first game it was clear that Ben was a hugely talented little footballer. He could shoot, tackle, dribble and head the ball like someone far beyond his years.

"At 15 I was one of the oldest but you always played fair. If you went in to a tackle with Ben and he got accidentally caught, he would get up, shake himself down and get on with the game, no moaning or seeking retribution. Within minutes he usually had his revenge by scoring a goal or going past you as though you weren't there.

"That summed Ben up for me. The cheeky little chap with short, spikey blond hair and an infectious grin who was a model sportsman.

"As time went on the sight of that legendary van brought smiles to the faces of everyone. It was more like a state visit than an evening at the park. Those few years growing up with those guys was a highlight for so many of us. It was sad when they came to an end."

From my personal point of view it was a privilege and a time I look back on with great affection, having made so many new friends and having received a vast amount of mutual trust and respect from all involved.

With Christmas upon us, the final touches were being made to both bedrooms, so with new beds plus carpets down they were both just about ready. There was a huge sigh of relief from Rachel, who at last had a mirror, a dressing table and sliding door wardrobe space. Her main ambition now was to fill it as quickly as possible with trendy clothing. Street cred was now becoming a priority.

This was something Father Christmas was well aware of. The rules still remained that we should meet up on the landing on Christmas morning before proceeding to the lounge to see if he had actually been. Even Gloria was allowed in first these days.

Poor Santa. He no longer was left a double whisky or a bar of chocolate to help him on his way. I thought this was very unjust.

It was strange, though, how we all still assembled at the most ridiculous hour of the morning yet the excitement and anticipation was the same it had always been, especially when the kids discovered most of their wish list had been delivered. So with Boxing Day and New Year's Eve celebrations still to come, it remained a very special time of the year for all of us.

Gloria remarked that the carpet (football pitch) in the hallway was looking worse for wear. I blamed the groundsman! But seriously, I knew urgent action was required.

The garage on the side of house was full of tables, chairs and other bits of furniture as well as tools and plant that I used for my job. Plan A was to board out the loft and transfer most of the items up there out of the way. Plan B then came into effect. With wood I often used in my job, I knocked up a table tennis board with two equal halves joined together with brass hinges which allowed it be folded away when not in use. I made some wooden legs to take the weight of the board, again with brass hinges, before hanging up a darts board and scoreboard complete with chalk all ready for play. Finally, I purchased a pool table with cues which all helped to create a mini games room.

This new room provided bags of entertainment during the darker evenings and our games options had increased, which we both enjoyed. On a slightly negative note, Gloria would not allow me to introduce a bar into the new room – although this was only required to celebrate or commiserate at the end of our games. Spoilsport!

Our first season in the Hanham Minor League proved to be very eventful. After a lot of thought, and for the overall benefit of the team, I decided to play Ben in the centre of midfield. His distribution of the ball was excellent, as was his ability to beat players with the ball at his feet. The fact he had an eye for goal and a deadly finish was a bonus for the team. Ben was happy with this and would never question my judgment. Like all the boys, he was happy just to be out on the pitch playing the game he loved.

In all we played 32 games, winning 20, losing seven and drawing five. We ended the season in fourth position, which I was very happy with. All the parents were very supportive and it was very much a team effort.

Ben not only scored 22 goals, he assisted in even more from his midfield position. In fact, along with his midfield partner Nicholas Rugman, the pair gave me firm belief we had the best midfield in the league.

We entered three six-a-side tournaments in the summer and reached the final of all of them, only to finish with a hat-trick of defeats. But my learning and knowledge of youth football was increasing and I found confidence was by some way the main factor in helping a lad improve their game, as well as enjoy it.

Personalities were different. Some boys needed a slightly more stern vocal approach when being coached, while others who were a little more nervous required a softer, more subtle approach. Personally I found that with confidence and trust, the boys expressed themselves in a positive way and always gave their best at training.

There were two teams in our league which stood out for me – Shirehampton Colts and Warmley Rangers, the latter managed by Gary Brindle. His boys won the league and set the standard for the rest of us. The way his lads passed and moved the ball was a credit to him and very much in the style of what I was trying to achieve at Stoke Lane. Now I was determined to reach and possibly surpass that level, so with the new season just around the corner, everyone was excited and full of optimism.

Our caravan was back on the road to Hoburne Park, Christchurch for the week. The evenings always started with bingo in the main clubroom, and if we got there early enough three of us would usually play – Rachel had secretly played many times before. However, for reasons unknown, Ben decided he would like to participate too, so Gloria and I kept a close eye on both their tickets, ready to take them if a full house were called. Talk about beginner's luck... On the final game of our book of five, Ben had a full house. Gloria duly shouted, and it was correct. I whispered to Ben to be silent, remain calm and just chill, which in fairness he did – although his face resembled a Cheshire cat. The drinks were definitely on him and, needless to say, bingo became the start of our evenings on this holiday.

This worked out nicely for the ladies as well. Ben and I would go to the club early so we could get a table close to the stage and dancefloor. The ladies would take an age getting ready and they often arrived at the bingo in the nick of time, just before it started. Mind you, they never missed it! In return I provided Ben with a little extra pocket money, no doubt for additional crisps or the arcade.

Later in the week, Ben took to the stage as he entered a competition to find the Hoburne Junior Prince. This involved young lads being asked various questions in an attempt to bring out their wit, charm and personality. Three judges from the audience were nominated to select the eventual winner. Because Ben was the fifth lad to come out onto the stage, he was already aware of the questions he was about to be asked, so he began with a one-liner that got the audience laughing. His confidence then grew and his other answers were more aimed at getting a laugh rather than honesty. The audience soon warmed to his humour and the fact he was one of the youngest to enter – along with his cheeky smile – certainly worked in his favour. By the time he had finished almost everyone was cheering, so the writing was on the wall. When he was announced as the winner, the reception he received certainly justified the judges' decision – especially when he went back on stage to receive his award. He returned home with a well-deserved plaque and medal for his efforts.

Trust Your Instincts

Our second season at Under-10 level started very positively as we won our first six games and sat proudly at the top of the league. A new player arrived and made his debut for us on December 5, 1993. Gary Warren went on to play in our final 13 games of the season. It soon became apparent that Gary, like Ben, was a special talent with similar attributes. He too had an abundance of skill and natural ability and was also able to score goals. He soon became an asset to the team.

Ben was very happy at Christmas that year as he got his own TV and video recorder – along with two of his favourite films: *Honey, I Shrunk The Kids*, which featured a guy he had previously liked from *Ghostbusters*, plus the first *Home Alone* movie, which cracked him up every time he saw it.

We also started off what was to become a huge collection of Bristol Rovers Screen Soccer videos. His first was *1990 Division Three Champions*. These videos come complete with commentary from Andy Warren and Dave Rodgers, whose voices are unmistakeable. Little did we know how often in the future we would hear their excited tones on a regular basis.

During February of this season at Stoke Lane, many parents made it clear to me that certain others were not happy with my team selections. They had even been offered the chance for their boy to play for a new team the other parents were looking to form next season, in opposition to us. This may have unsettled some of the boys, but my conscience was clear so I carried on exactly as before. We finished the season in third place after 26 games – winning 19, losing five and drawing two. I was well satisfied with this, having witnessed much improvement from most of the boys.

Ben was once again voted player of the year by the parents. We entered two summer six-a-side tournaments and reached the final of the first one – only to lose out yet again, this time to Shirehampton Colts. The second one was played at Warmley on June 26, 1994 – six days after Ben's 10th birthday. And what a nice belated present it was. We won a cup final for the first time on a hot and humid day, ending the season exactly how we had started it – on top.

Chapter Six

FLYING HIGH

T his was to be our last season in the Hanham Minor League and, as expected, a few players had to leave. But two new lads – Matthew Carroll and Jon Balsdon – came to join us from Shirehampton, where apparently they were not required. Chris Barrass came along as our new goalkeeper, replacing Andrew Jones – who proved his versatility by claiming his place as a defender. Dominic Sutherland and a lad similar in stature to Ben – Craig Lanfear – also came along. Our midfield engine room now saw a slight change with Gary Warren partnering Ben, which made it even stronger – a source of confidence for all around. The task now was to see how all the lads gelled together. The season ahead looked interesting.

The two bedrooms at home were now becoming more popular yet different in their own ways. Rachel naturally enjoyed the privacy of her own room – as did Ben in his. But the noise level from the guys left nothing to the imagination about what was going on up there. While it was good to hear them sharing fun and laughter, shouting up the stairs to ask them to calm down and lower the volume became a regular thing. Needless to say the ladies were a lot more discreet, often having to remind the guys about their manners.

As for me, my cooking skills were now being put to the test. As long as I arrived home at a decent hour, I would prepare and cook our meals. This is something I enjoy and after a hard day's graft, I find it therapeutic – and Gloria certainly has no problems with it.

Having been used to cook a similar type of meal for the four of us, my flexibility was now being tested. The guys were easy, never too fussy. As long as chips, burgers, pizza or chicken nuggets were involved somewhere along the line, they were content. Likewise with desserts – ice cream, trifle, cheesecake or anything involving chocolate was all well greeted.

The young ladies, however, were a little more particular. They wanted fresh salads, roasted or steamed veg, grilled meats or jacket potatoes. Now even the capabilities of the cooker were under scrutiny with the rings, grill, oven and the microwave all very active. The kitchen became a hot place to be, although I did get used to it after a while and just took it all with a pinch of salt.

Ben was now well into his final year at junior school and we were very satisfied with his progress. His teachers were very much of the same opinion. At infant level, Miss Lane followed Mrs Callow, while at juniors it was Mrs Lewis, Mrs Jardin and Mrs Davies. After meeting with all of them periodically, it became clear Ben was an active class member always willing to offer his services. He was very popular among his classmates and usually at the centre of most group activities. We were made aware that he was particularly good at maths, which was encouraging. At home we noted that that he was usually happy when he came home after school, more often than not with plans of his own which invariably involved his friends.

At the end of the season the boys exceeded my expectations. We played 30 games and finished fourth in the league, winning 17, losing 10 and drawing three. We also had a really good cup run, making it to the semi-finals before losing narrowly to old foes Shirehampton.

On Sunday, July 9, 1995 we went down to the Scotch Horn playing fields at Nailsea and duly won the six-a-side tournament, yet again on a hot summer's day.

During the spring of that year, Ben joined Bradley Stoke Cricket Club. Yet again, he was one of the youngest to represent the club since it started at Under-13 level. One home game against Charfield saw him pick up the man of the match award after he took five wickets for four runs and was consequently carried shoulder high from the field surrounded by cheering team-mates. The game took place on June 19, one day before his 11th birthday. Shortly afterwards he received a unique memento from the game – the ball with which he took his wickets mounted on a plaque stand.

The end of term was quite a sad day at school. Some friends would be moving to Filton High, while others would be going to other local senior schools. Some of them would stay in touch via football, cricket or the local park. But for many it was a big farewell.

Our experiences in the caravan were so popular we decided to invest in an Elddis Wisp van along with an awning, which when fitted would double the size of the caravan. We headed down to Sandford Park near Poole, Dorset. Shortly after our arrival, Rachel and Ben disappeared, which was the start of a regular disappearing act. You see, once the caravan was stationary and in its correct position, levelling it was a piece of cake. But you needed to be an octopus to connect the awning to the side of van, and a humid day or evening was certainly not a good time to attempt this. It was one of the rare times Gloria and I exchanged words – not very nice ones! And it was strange how once the job was finally completed, the young ones would suddenly show up again with big smiles on their faces. I'm glad someone had enjoyed themselves.

The facilities on offer at the park soon made it a favourite of ours. Poole Harbour became the location for our crabbing, although now this took place later in the mornings – and even Gloria would join us sometimes. Sandbanks was also nearby, which provided a nice beach for swimming, sunbathing and our usual games, although by this time they were usually an all-male affair.

There was, however, one game that all four of us enjoyed. Sandbanks boasted an immaculate putting green, which became popular with all of us. To their credit, Gloria Rachel and Ben not only enjoyed playing but all improved their games along the way. We played one or very often two rounds of 18 holes with cash for the winner – although even as the provider of this, I was exempt from winning it. My job was to play and also mark the scorecards. It was well worth it though. Thanks to my winding up here and there, the mood at times became quite heated. I provided live commentary throughout our games, which often unsettled one or two and added some pressure on all three to succeed – especially with bragging rights at stake as well as cash. Come the end, all three would wait nervously while I took an age to add the scores up (accidentally on purpose). Whatever the outcome, it was always great fun – or at least I thought so!

As well as bingo and a couple of other competitions, our evenings now included a spot of disco dancing thanks to a DJ. Miraculously, after a few beverages, I found that I could boogie better than ever, despite sarcastic remarks from certain quarters which were no doubt payback for some of my wind-ups. Oh well, it's no good giving it if you can't take it.

There was an early surprise for Ben on his induction day at Filton High School, when all the new pupils gathered to be introduced to their new tutors. Later in the day, the most popular boy and girl would be given the title of head for the year, but this could only be done via nominations so all the pupils could vote. Ben was nominated by some of his classmates, who had also been to Little Stoke Juniors. Others who voted in his favour included a lad from Filton Hill Juniors. As Matthew Walker recalls: "I was fond of two things when I first became aware of Ben on day one – his Kickers school shoes and the greased centre-parting in his hair. We soon struck up an instant friendship."

The announcement at the end of voting confirmed that Ben was head boy for the year.

As the football season started at Under-12 level in the Avon Youth League, it became apparent among all teams that some lads were maturing more quickly than others. We were lacking a little additional strength and although it was only a short-term thing, it was making a difference. We lost our first three games before recovering well and winning the next three. New lad Kevin Gray joined our ranks to give us a boost.

Part of the way through the season I received a call from Bristol Rovers Youth Academy who enquired about Ben and whether I could bring him along to training. When I put it to him he was excited, so for the rest of the season I took him one night a week to train with the academy under floodlights at the Sun Life HQ at Cribbs Causeway.

When school ended, Ben had a regular partner to accompany him back home. Chris Church really relished spending time together with Ben and they loved to play Championship Manager on the computer – in between raiding the Hiscox sweet cupboard!

Chris says: "There were more sweets there than in the local shops! The chocolate was great and it gave us lots of energy to play our favourite game. It was madness but great fun." Since attending Filton High, the two had become even closer as mates.

Thanks to some of his new schoolmates, Ben became aware of The Pyramid Youth Club in Filton Avenue and went there two nights a week. It soon became a big favourite, especially after making even more new friends. Whilst at the club over a period of many months, he took on a series of activities before gaining the Duke of Edinburgh's Bronze Award, which was aimed at giving service to others. Past experiences in our own games room paid dividends when he represented the club at table tennis and pool against other local youth clubs. They were also looking to start up a football team, something else he became quite excited about.

Considering our slow start, I was really pleased as our season came to an end. We played 22 games, winning 11, losing eight and drawing three to finish in fourth position once again. Towards the end of the season we gained two interesting new arrivals in Jordan Murdoch and Gib Keicht, both lads being made very welcome. They showed a lot of ability, as well as providing that bit of physical strength that we lacked. Hopefully next season could now be very interesting.

The news was not so good for Ben at Bristol Rovers. Although they were pleased with his progress, they decided not to retain him. It seemed that once again his age – and more particularly his size – had gone against him.

On a more positive note, Ben's friendship with schoolmate Adam Thorne worked in our favour. Adam's grandparents Mike and Sandy, who managed the local Parkway Tavern pub, took a shine to Ben and soon became part of our team at Stoke Lane. Not only did they provide the boys with complete new kit and training tops, they also provided for our own use a large function room at the pub which we could use when we wanted, completely free of charge. We did have to purchase our own drinks at the bar though! Mike and Sandy were very popular among the locals thanks to their warm and friendly welcome. We soon got to discover why.

At school a varied group of lads were beginning to form friendships with Ben. Lunchtimes over in the fields were especially welcomed by Pierre Renee, who loved a kickabout and a game of Wembley. He says: "To play alongside Ben at lunch was great. I played for fun, I was never going to break into a team. But every time we played it seemed impossible to get the ball off Ben with his close dribbling skills. You never really knew just how good you had to be to break into the professional ranks, but in my eyes he was crazy good!"

While consuming lunch, Matthew Walker just had to stop and stare. He recalls: "Ben used to lick the hell out of his crisps before fully eating them. I found this odd yet entertaining."

The group was slowly increasing in number and although it was early days, friendships were growing. Only time would tell how close they would become.

Good News For The Gas

The County Ground home of Gloucestershire Cricket Club became a very popular venue for Ben that summer. He became a season ticket-holder for the first time and later played a game at the ground. Along with Gary Warren, the two had a good season playing for Old Down Cricket Club. They even made it through to the final of the cup, which was staged at the County Ground. Their opponents were top-of-the-league Rockhampton and a very tight game swung one way and then the other before Old Down ran out winners, to the jubilation of all the boys. It was a great advert for youth cricket.

Sandford Park in Dorset was acting like a magnet for our caravan whenever holidays came around. One visit saw us meet up again with a good friend we had met a few years earlier while on holiday in Cornwall.

Top comedian and impressionist Paul Burling was head of the entertainment team at the campsite, ensuring the days and evenings were fun filled.

The activities one day included an adult football competition, so Ben and I went along. Paul met everyone wearing his beloved Liverpool kit. He was representing the entertainment team while the rest of us campers were split into three other teams, which led to two semi-final matches. We both started our first game playing together in midfield and it worked really well, as we won the game. Ben's energy and natural talent stood out like a sore thumb while I won and distributed the ball quite well. We won the final and came out of both games with much credit from our team-mates, which was really nice.

Yet it was to get even better during the evening when several of us met up again in the club. Compliments about our performances came flying our way from many of the guys, with one even asking me which team I played for back home!

At the end of the evening and after many refreshments, the four of us started walking back to our caravan and I announced that I might start playing football again. Gloria just laughed loudly at this so I replied angrily: "No, seriously!"

The following morning my head was thumping. But worse, my joints and muscles were aching like mad. In fact, I was so stiff I could barely get out of bed. As hard as I tried, I couldn't disguise the fact that moving was painful, so I just sat down and waited for the inevitable onslaught. The ladies were far less forgiving than Ben, who just asked: "OK dad, whose it going to be – Rovers or Tottenham?" He was chuckling to himself but at least he left it there. As for the girls, my woes gave them ammunition for many days of jibes and laughs at my expense.

The evenings, however, gave all four of us the biggest laughs watching Paul carry out his act, which is always hilarious. My joints did not approve but it was well worth it – something we all agreed on.

Great news came about when it was revealed that Bristol Rovers were ending their exile in Bath – they had been sharing Bath City's Twerton Park ground – and returning to Bristol to be tenants of Bristol Rugby Club at the Memorial Ground. This was an exciting time for many people, including Ben, who had a new Rovers shirt and his first season ticket. He was eagerly awaiting the start of the new season.

Striker Chris Johnston and defender Joel Swire joined us for the new season, which started on Sunday, September 15, 1996 against big rivals Shirehampton. Although we lost 1-0 I firmly believed the result flattered them and we went unbeaten for the next seven games. Then came the acid test – the return fixture at Shirehampton. We won 2-1 and did so comfortably. This was a huge turning point in our season – certainly no fluke, and my own thoughts were now firmly on reigning champions Warmley. Later I realised that our final two games of the season would be against them. Ouch!

Ben's growing group of friends at school did not just include lads. Katie Gleeson became a good friend and the two of them spent a lot of time together, including Christmas Day after repeated requests to both families. Sally Young was suffering with "lady problems" and Becci Davison remembers Ben trying to cheer her up by making a joke about how many periods he had at school every day!

Teacher Tom Watson said: "Ben is a very upbeat, lively (in the best sense of the word) young man who always wants to work hard but have fun at the same time."

His character was beginning to have an effect on those around him and it usually provided most with a big smile.

As well as doing well in the league, we were making progress in the cup and reached the semi-final against Avon Athletic, which was a real family affair as they were managed by none other than John Gibbs, so

Ben would be playing against his cousin Wayne. Bragging rights were now up for grabs.

It was a close, passionate game which we won 2-1. We all celebrated like mad, and rightly so, as we had reached the final for the first time. But the banter didn't really kick off. If you have a lot in common — especially when it's family and fellow Gasheads — then it's best just left.

After that game, we carried on in the league in much the same style, winning our next six games. This left us with just three games to play, with our cup final appearance sandwiched in between home and away games against Warmley which would decide who finished as champions.

Gloria's love of Cannon and Ball had now dwindled, but her new love was now singer and impressionist Joe Longthorne. When Gloria believes in something, she never does things in half measures. Not only did she follow his career closely but she became a member of his fan club and would find out where and when he was performing. She often went off to see him performing live and would sometimes stop off overnight if the venue was further afield. She even got to organise trips with close friends, many of who became fan club members too.

I always had a tongue-in-cheek smile when her lovely friends arrived at our house dressed to the nines and with bunches of flowers to give to Joe. By the time they left, the car would look like a delivery vehicle from a florist!

If the shows included an overnight stay then Rachel would often go too — and this is where my lack of understanding of video technology nearly embarrassed me big time. I would always be asked if I could record certain programmes on different channels while they were away. (Surely, apart from *Match of the Day*, what else is worth watching?)

If the truth be known, I didn't have a clue how to do this. But I knew someone who did. Ben always set up the recordings for me and was always spot on. He never let me down. I always returned the favour by nipping out to our favourite Ko Sing House takeaway before returning with a lush curry just in time to watch *Match Of The Day* together. Of course, he was well aware that mum was the word and it took a long time before the truth came to light. Nice one mate!

Just before our final three games of the season we went on a five-day spring tour to Wall Park in Brixham, Devon, where we would be playing against a variety of other teams from across the south-west. Although it was very tiring as we played two games a day, we ended up being tournament winners – excellent preparation for our final three games.

On the evening of Thursday, April 10, 1997 we were at home to Warmley and appeared to be carrying on in exactly the same manner. We were 2-1 up with five minutes left and looking comfortable. But in the final minute we conceded an equaliser and, deep into stoppage time, Warmley scored again with the very last kick of the game. It was unbelievable that we actually ended up losing 3-2 and all the boys were shattered and quite distraught.

It was my job to pick them back up again and what happened in the changing room gave me a huge amount of encouragement. While I was reflecting on our display in a positive manner, many of the boys took it upon themselves to apologise for their errors with certain individuals wanting to take the blame for our defeat. Of course, I was having none of it but at least it showed the sort of team spirit we had developed.

Sunday, April 20 was cup final day at the Sun Life Stadium at Cribbs Causeway. We were facing St Vallier on a very heavy pitch. Dominic scored an absolute cracker to put us ahead but shortly afterwards Jordan clashed with his team-mate Kevin as they both jumped for a high ball. It was purely accidental but the collision broke Jordan's nose. Worse was to follow when Chris Johnston broke away but went down after a challenge and ended up breaking his arm in two places. He was whisked away in an ambulance but within minutes St Vallier equalised.

As the game wore on, the conditions took their toll on both sides. Ben's workrate in the middle of the park was immense and he was never far away from the action, wherever on the pitch it was.

Extra time failed to separate the teams so it all came down to a dreaded penalty shoot-out. Lady Luck was on our side and we won 4-2.

But although it was a memorable day for us, it was tinged with sadness for Jordan and Chris, who would both miss our final game the following Sunday.

We went over to Warmley to play that game at Cadbury Heath's ground. It was a big pitch and we had to soak up a lot of pressure in the first half, but we fought like tigers to go in 0-0 at the break.

Luck was with us again in the second half when one of their lads missed a penalty. Shortly afterwards, Kevin Gray scored with a header to give us the lead. The next few lines are copied from my first book which contained the match report from the day.

"With seven minutes remaining, Ben received the ball. There was not much on but to his credit, he beat three players before chipping the ball over their goalkeeper for a memorable goal."

We went on to win the game 2-0 and finish as champions, which gave me immense pride and pleasure.

My final analysis of the season, again taken from my book, reads: All this success is thanks to the sheer teamwork, effort and commitment from the boys. I am so proud of each and every one of them because in the end, they all did themselves justice. What a great bunch of lads."

For me, those words summed everything up perfectly.

On the very last page of my first book – dated Monday, April 28, 1997 – I ended with these words: "This book represents the end of an era – good times, bad times, happy and sad. It has formed a large part of my life and I would not change it for anything – maybe perhaps with a little less heartache but I am sure experience will see to that. Thankfully Ben started out as a star, carried on as a star and finished as a star – a true star. I hope and pray it continues into my next book. For all his effort and determination, he deserves that at the very least."

My next book was now ready and waiting for our Under-14 campaign.

Apart from crossing the border into Wales, we had never been abroad – mainly due to Gloria's fear of flying. All that changed as she approached her 50th birthday. "It's now or never," she said, and consequently booked us a holiday in Majorca to stay at the Continental Apartments in Alcudia.

Rachel was now at an age where she wanted to do her own thing so the three of us jetted off on our maiden flight, which we all enjoyed – leaving two of us to wonder why we hadn't done it before.

The apartments surrounded an inviting swimming pool while the beach and plenty of tavernas were close at hand. Ben dined out with us on our first night, but that was to be the only time as he soon made friends with some other lads staying in the apartments, which saw him part of a group of four. Daytimes for them were either spent around the pool or in the large games room underneath the apartments with the occasional visit to the beach.

In the evenings, tavernas were replaced by a visit to a KFC or the burger bar opposite the apartments. Our stay seemed to fly by but we all really enjoyed it. On our way home, the question was whether that would be our last flight. I wonder...

Chapter Seven

PART-TIME WORK BEGINS

A s well as renewing his season ticket at Rovers, Ben also wanted to travel to a lot of away games, so Gloria got into the habit of booking him a seat on coach one. She would then drop him and a mate off at the Memorial Ground early on Saturday mornings. He soon got to know a lot of the regulars on the coach, especially four older ladies who always sat in the same seats up the front. He struck up a friendship with them and found them fascinating characters. Apparently they had been staunch supporters and regulars on the coach for many years, so he too was now looking to become part of the elite.

Following our success the previous season, we were now the team to beat. Gary and Jordan were not available some weeks because they had been accepted into the youth academy teams at Bristol Rovers and Swindon Town respectively. However, we did gain three accomplished new lads in Tom Collett, Grant Gordon and Andrew Proctor to help us defend our titles.

We were certainly in no mood to give them up easily. We only lost one of our first eight league games, while in the cup we were progressing towards the final again having beaten Shirehampton, Warmley and two others.

At school, Ben was developing a reputation which one teacher in particular enjoyed. Esther Keller – better known as Mrs PK – taught sociology and English. She said: "His good nature, smile and sparkling presence were a delight for any teacher. He is always so positive and polite, I genuinely enjoy teaching him. If all pupils were like him, teachers would have a brilliant time every lesson."

Sport-loving Danny Leach became a good mate. He played cricket in the same school team and became a Gashead after visiting the Memorial Ground with his friend. Danny said: "I found Ben to be a true friend who always put others first. He never speaks ill of anyone. He's always smiling and great fun to be with."

The young man was certainly becoming popular!

Having just won our semi-final, we were through to the final of the cup for the second year running and would face Brislington. We had already beaten them twice in the league – 5-1 away and 3-2 at home in a game where Ben scored two amazing individual goals, similar to the one at Warmley the previous season. His main contribution this season, however, was the amount of assists he was making. He developed a quite unique understanding with Chris Johnston, who was now back with us and scoring goals for fun. A defining moment in our season came on Sunday, February 1, 1998 away to Warmley. We not only won 5-0 but did it comfortably.

The ladies on the coach to Rovers' away games had by now become even more popular with Ben, who nicknamed them "The Golden Girls". They became his minders on away trips. Unbeknown to Ben, Gloria met up with Sylvia, Freda, Jean and Joan, who had really taken to him. They assured her that he was kept under their wing and they always looked after him during their travels. Gloria was very thankful to all of them as it did provide us with peace of mind.

By early April, we had still only lost one game but bad news was to follow off the pitch. Ben had an accident, broke his wrist and was likely to miss the few remaining games of the season.

Sunday, April 26, 1998 saw us return to the Sun Life Stadium for our second cup final. A rollercoaster game was deadlocked at 2-2 after extra time, so we had to endure another penalty shoot-out. Luck deserted us this time, however, as we lost it 5-4. But we did win our final game of the season, played on Sunday, May 10, which ensured we finished as champions for the second year running. Having lost only twice, this game saw Ben make a substitute appearance – so at least he was back in the fold ready for the next season.

It was a big day and a big game at school as the teachers prepared to take on the pupils in a cricket match. Mr McDermott, head of PE, spiced things up when he told the boys: "No-one will get me out!", which only served to make them even more determined to do so. As the game progressed, the teachers were knocking up a big score and confidence was low among the boys, especially when Mr McDermott came to the crease to bat. Shortly after, Ben took his turn to bowl – and hit the jackpot! He clean bowled him before running down the wicket to do a roly poly. His fellow pupils mobbed him in delight.

The teachers ended up convincing winners but it was especially nice for the pupils when Mr McDermott later went over to acknowledge Ben, giving him a pat on the back and saying: "Well done, young man!" Fellow team-mate Danny Leach was well impressed.

With the new season about to start, Bristol Rovers became proud ground owners. Due to financial difficulties, Bristol Rugby Club decided to sell the ground to their tenants, although both clubs would continue to share it. However, the ground was renamed and now became the Memorial Stadium, home of Bristol Rovers FC. After encouragement from Ben, a couple of his schoolmates collected their season tickets too. Now they were all ready and waiting for the start of the season.

It was all systems go on the flying front, albeit still with caution – so the relatively short flight to Majorca was again the favoured choice. This time it was to Cala Bona, staying at the Bonaire Aparthotel, which provided excellent facilities with plenty of day and night entertainment.

Within a day of our arrival, Ben met another lad from Stoke. Within a couple of days, the two became 12. As a group, they named themselves Generation X, apparently something to do with the wrestling scene, which was popular. When the lads met up each day their greeting was to cross their arms forming an X. I found it strange, yet in fairness they stayed together throughout the holiday. They shared fun and a bit of ribbing together, often trying to outdo each other during teenage games, which meant they had to take to the stage. One record which saw them all take to the dancefloor was the Baddiel and Skinner *Three Lions 98* song, which was England's theme tune at the World Cup. The group became inseparable and it was quite sad when we boarded the coach to go back to the airport. All the lads stood with their arms firmly crossed to wish Ben farewell as we pulled away.

Once we were back home, he did stay in touch with his pal from Stoke and made a few trips via train to meet up with him, which included going to watch Port Vale, his mate's favourite team.

Within two months of our return, Gloria had booked another holiday abroad for the following year. This meant our caravan was surplus to requirements – another farewell soon followed.

Gary and Jordan were still restricted in the number of games they would be available as our season got underway at Under-15 level. We welcomed one new arrival, Nick Stewart – and on his debut on September 6, 1998 he scored five goals for us as we looked to carry on from where we left off the season before.

The lads were now at an age where I was able to switch things around tactically at will. Full credit to them for performing with confidence and playing as a unit, whichever roles I asked them to play. The season ahead looked very interesting.

Ben was on the lookout for a little part-time job, but since it was his first he was reluctant to start alone. I was not keen on him taking a door-to-door delivery job with another mate, so it was interesting one evening when we visited our local chippy after football training. We got to know both the young men who cooked and worked behind the counter. We often shared a joke or a leg-pull after placing our order.

As it happened, Chris Church lived near the chip shop and he became aware they wanted someone to work a couple of evenings. It worked out perfectly and it was agreed that both lads could start working two evenings a week between 5pm and 8pm. Their main job was to peel the potatoes ready for the chip machine.

Shortly after that a format came into place at the end of school. As before, Chris would accompany Ben home, this time though to grab a snack before going off to work. He was always excited about this, especially since Ben had introduced him to what became a favourite food of theirs – super noodles! The pair would simply devour them before setting off as new employees of the Frying machine, based in north Bradley Stoke. It was all go nowadays for these two young men.

So Proud Of My Boys!

While standing among the regulars at the Blackthorn End of the Memorial Stadium, Ben was starting to use his vocal chords to start many varied footy songs aimed at encouraging the players. He was usually joined by the majority of fans behind the goalmouth, which gave him lots of satisfaction, helping to create an atmosphere which all the fans enjoyed. The bigger the response, the bigger the smile on his face.

On Saturday evenings there would often be a similar pattern of conversation as we discussed the day's game. Ben would always refer to a certain part of the match when Rovers had carried out some neat interplay or had a near miss on goal. He would then ask if I remembered a certain song or chorus which followed that piece of action and had all the fans singing along too. With a big grin he assured me that he was the one who had started that crescendo of noise, as well as other songs at certain points in the game. Returning his smile, I assured him that the choir had sounded really good and that it was a nice way of showing support for the team.

The season was building to an exciting climax at Stoke Lane. Having lost our semi-final in the cup during extra time, the league title went right down to our final game – and what a thriller it was. Our opponents were Shirehampton, who we had beaten 4-1 earlier in the season. But we weren't kidding ourselves that this game would be a formality – and we weren't wrong.

Early in the game we found ourselves a goal down, although we did equalise just before half time. Shortly into the second half, we went 2-1 down and things were not looking good. But with 10 minutes to go, Ben produced a bit of magic yet again. After receiving the ball, he attacked and beat two players before releasing the ball perfectly to the onrushing Chris Johnston, who finished the move for our equaliser.

The Shirehampton goalmouth was now being bombarded – but just when it looked as though the clock was going to deny us, we scored in the last minute to win the game. This was the third season running we had finished as champions and boy, what a feeling! The lads had done me proud again.

I did not realise that day – April 25, 1999 – would be my last game as manager of Stoke Lane. After weeks of careful thought and consideration, I felt that I had surpassed the level that I had set out to achieve many years before. This, along with the amount of my time it was consuming, led me to my decision. Nearly everyone was astonished when I told them of my intention – everyone bar one, the person who knew me best. Poor Gloria was now faced with the prospect of having me around more often.

Since officially starting out at Under-9 level, we had played 170 games, won 112, lost 37 and drew 21. I consider myself privileged to have coached 42 boys and sincerely hope I may have helped each of them to improve and enjoy their own game, eventually being a better player for it. As the only original from beginning to the end, Ben played 164 games and scored 63 goals from his midfield position. I could not keep count of the number of assists he made.

Once he was aware of my decision, he was really surprised – and yet not long afterwards, he decided it might be a good time to enter the world of adult football. What he had to consider was what level to start at and for which team – hopefully one that was local.

Close friend Gary Warren was quite sad when he heard the news about Stoke Lane and the fact he would no longer be playing alongside his mate. He reflected: "Ben and I struck up an instant friendship when we first met as young kids playing football for Stoke Lane. We played together from Under-9s to Under-15s and formed a formidable midfield partnership. For me, this was the start of so many happy childhood memories.

"I will always remember after our games the lunches at the Hiscox household. I would try to make up any excuse not to go back to my mum's for dinner so I could go back with Ben to Clive and Gloria's. We would have pizza, crisps, sandwiches, chocolate – it was a young kid's dream food. We would demolish this then go out in the afternoon for a football match down at the fields or cricket in the back garden. It was awesome!"

Going back to Stoke Lane, Gary added: "I ran around a lot while Ben bamboozled the opposition with his cheekiness and cheesy smile! Seriously though, he was the glue that held our youth teams together. I could never understand why he was never given a chance by a professional club. Who knows what might have happened. Ben being Ben, he would not have been bothered by that. He was just happy to play the game with his mates and enjoy himself."

Gary is currently playing in the Scottish Premier League for Inverness Caledonian Thistle.

The pair of them remained together throughout the summer months as cricket took centre stage. Outstanding batting and bowling from them saw Old Down win the league at Under-15 level. When they were not playing they were usually watching Gloucestershire, either at the County Ground or other parts of the country via the train. There were trips to Worcestershire, Leicestershire and Lord's, the home of Middlesex. These came complete with bat and ball, full packed lunch boxes and a couple of cans of Foster's borrowed from home. The long days provided much fun and enjoyment, which they both loved.

First Girlfriend

Our holiday that year took us to Porto Rico in Gran Canaria. We stayed at the Eden Apartments close to the commercial centre, which hosted lots of bars and restaurants. One evening we were going out to wine and dine and I wanted to wear my new blue shirt but couldn't find it. I asked Gloria if she had packed it but she apologised, saying she thought she had. It was no big deal.

On our way back, we passed a bar with a big dancefloor playing really loud music. In the distance was a large group of guys of different shapes and sizes dancing in a circle. An opening appeared, and in the middle was a small lad with a pint glass raised in one hand while the other was punching the air. The song being played was *Mambo No. 5* by Lou Bega.

The lad was very smartly dressed in trousers and a blue shirt. From a distance he even looked similar to Ben. With a smile on my face, I mentioned this to Gloria, who decided to walk along the dancefloor to take a closer look. On her return she revealed that it was Ben – and it looked like he was dancing for England! Rather than embarrass him, we carried on back to our apartment for some much-needed sleep.

A little while later we became aware of his return so I jumped out of bed to check out his condition. In a loud voice and with a huge grin, my greeting was standard: "Alright dad, how ya doing?" … although it was slurred. "I'm good thanks mate," was my reply, which was then followed by a full-blown conversation on how the events of the evening had gone. It sounded like great fun until Gloria shouted for silence and an immediate return to bed.

An hour or so later, the price of the fun – and the intake of alcohol – was being paid. The bathroom remained busy with constant visits with Gloria keeping him company, as mum's often do in these circumstances.

For Ben, the following day was spent mainly in bed. This was the first time he had experienced the effects of excessive alcohol. Hopefully the lesson would be learned. He did express the usual words prompted by his condition: "Never again!"

That was certainly the case for the remainder of the holiday. Unknown to him, I played the role of minder, keeping a check on his friends and drink. The pint had been replaced by a small bottle of alcopop.

Throughout the holiday, Ben's popularity with the other guys increased. This became even more evident on our last night following a visit to the commercial centre. He was the leader of the pack with all the other guys following, trying to imitate his every move. The song blasting out was Ricky Martin's *Livin' La Vida Loca*. In fairness, the rest did not seem bothered about the fact they were following and copying the smallest member of the group. They were all out for a good time, which is what they were having judging by their faces. Ben returned to the apartment later happy but with a tinge of sadness, having said farewell to his mates. The plane journey home would provide him with time to reflect on the whole experience – no doubt accompanied by a grin or two.

Having recently stopped his part-time job at the chip shop, Ben needed a boost to his pocket money so he applied for and got a part-time job at the Next warehouse in Patchway, working two evenings a week. He seemed to enjoy his new job, especially after making a few new friends. He even let it slip that one of them was very special indeed – a girlfriend that he had pulled! Interesting.

Social time was beginning to be spent more with Adam at the Parkway Tavern, although it soon became apparent that it wasn't just Adam's company he was enjoying. Ben started collecting empty glasses from the tables and returning them to the bar. Mike and Sandy found this helpful so they often rewarded him with a glass of cola. He also enjoyed exchanging comments with some of the customers sat around the tables. The regulars soon became aware of his presence and recognised a bit of a character in their verbal exchanges. The comical banter between them increased and usually included a bit of leg pulling and good humour as they got to know each other better.

It was Christmas party time at school and for most it would be the last, so everyone was out and up for a good time, socialising and enjoying each other's company. It's always too soon when it ends so, along with Chris and Adam, Ben decided to keep the feel good factor going by heading into town, ending up at The Mandrake pub. Later, the three of them somehow made it back to our home and into Ben's room, where he fell straight to sleep. Between them they somehow managed to shave off one of Ben's eyebrows for a joke before Adam was sick on the floor. Within minutes they both joined Ben for a snoring contest.

When she discovered them the next morning, Gloria went into a mode of ranting and raving at the guys, who both looked bemused and shameful. Later, she could see that they were genuinely worried by their actions, so she calmed down a little bit. By the time they were ready to depart, we could all see the funny side of things. Hopefully it was a lesson learned.

As a checkout operator at the local Tesco, Gloria had a huge amount of customers she had befriended. With her genuine, warm and welcoming personality, customers of all ages found it easy to converse with her while passing through her till. Many would keep a lookout to see which till she was operating.

One morning an elderly lady came through her till. She was also a bubbly character and after an initial greeting and a bit of a tongue wag, it became apparent her name was Barbara. She also revealed that she worked at Next in Patchway and, with a broad smile on her face, confided that she had a charming young boyfriend whose name just happened to be…Ben!

His charm and wit remained very popular among his mates at school. Matthew explains: "Somehow he had the ability to charm and cheek our teachers and get away with it every time!"

Andy Peters was sat around a table with Mr Bennett discussing GCSE exams. Ben asked if he got a D in one subject and a J in another, did that mean he could become a DJ? The one-liner brought smiles to all around.

Christina Davies was also impressed with her mate. "Whenever I think of Ben I simply smile. He is always so so positive, kind and humble with a great sense of humour, always cracking jokes. I love his wide smile and shiny blue eyes. It's always comforting to see."

The group, which by now had been long established, enjoyed sharing their own company. Ben was even arriving at school earlier than usual. Chris had recently acquired a moped so he allowed Ben to jump on the back before racing through the village in double quick time. Slow down!

Having become popular with the regulars at the Parkway Tavern, Ben had by now become a regular himself, often alone when visiting and collecting glasses from the tables while sharing a bit of friendly banter.

One evening a new face entered the Tavern and, after an initial meeting, made a good impression on Ben. He soon became acquainted with Gemma Walker. Both found they had a lot in common, including musical tastes as well as a sense of humour. The pair really hit it off as mates and agreed to meet up on a more regular basis, which they did. Soon afterwards, Gemma introduced a few of her own mates so Ben soon got to know Hannah, Jenny and Amy very well. They spent a lot of time together and he became the token boy in the group. A typical evening would see him call on the girls before proceeding into the village, often calling at the Tavern where a pint of cola was always made to last – sometimes with the added luxury of a bag of crisps.

All the girls loved his company, and especially his sense of humour, which often had them in stitches. They were all part of a friendly group. At the end of the evening, as a gentleman, he would often walk them back to their homes – although not always. Sometimes the roles were reversed – lucky lad!

Chapter Eight

TWO NEW TEAMS

T he search for a local team became quite hard for Ben. Stoke Gifford played in a high-standard league and although they had a reserve side, the club was traditional – very much a closed unit for the tried and trusted, which offered less opportunities for local youngsters.

Local store M&Ws, along with a few other shops, was centrally based in the village of Stoke Gifford. It became a prime meeting place for youngsters with its open space making it very popular. Local lad Lawrence Benson approached the area one day to witness a large group of teenagers milling around. He vaguely recognised some of them, having attended St Michael's Primary School locally, although he ended up going to The Ridings Secondary School, whereas most of the lads present were from Filton High.

However, among the youthful crowd he noticed Ben, who was hanging back from the main group. He was holding a packet of crisps while kicking a football around under the roofed area, along with a younger boy. Lawrence became intrigued by the playful nature of this teenager, spending time away from his peers to entertain a younger kid, knocking the ball past him and using the angles of the walls to keep hold of it whilst the boy hopelessly chased his shadow. After a request to find out who he was, Lawrence became aware that the teenager in question was Ben Hiscox. The surname was familiar to him, having maintained a love-hate relationship with Ben's cousins Lloyd and Gavin until they had moved to Bournemouth a few years earlier. Walking away from the group, the thought played on his mind: "Yet another Hiscox. Hmmm... interesting!"

For all those leaving school, the final day brought a bittersweet feeling. Most would be moving on with their lives in a new direction without the ones they had shared it with over the past five years. Although it was a happy time for many, for others it was a time for reflection.

Teacher Sarah Turner says: "In my time at Filton High I met thousands of students. Ben will always remain in my memory as a pleasant, positive young man without an ounce of malice. Everything he did was approached with enthusiasm. I especially liked his smile.

Good mate Matthew says: "I always liked Ben for his wit and charm – a very attractive person to be around. He was the alternative Robin Hood of Filton High, the guy that would always lend you £2 whilst pinching £3 from your other coat pocket."

Ben had made and gained many good friends from school. He was looking to keep in touch with most, although his priority now was a career – something he was undecided about.

It was thanks to another mate, this time from the Tavern, that Ben became aware of a new football team. Jamie White invited him to join the side which had recently been set up by his dad Errol, the aptly named Parkway Tavern FC. The team had started out the season before but many players had departed so now they were on the lookout for new ones.

Pre-season training had been arranged at Mead Park on the north edge of Gifford, so Ben went along hoping to be part of the new team.

It was here he first came face to face with Lawrence Benson, an original team member who had played the season before. Lawrence was a decent player but sensed a bit of rivalry coming up against yet another Hiscox. This became even more apparent during training when they played in opposite teams, both looking to prove their capabilities against each other just to see who could come out on top.

Ben's request for a mate to join him on holiday was turned down, although secretly we did have sympathy for his case. So two months after his 16th birthday, the three of us were off to San Antonio Bay in Ibiza. We stayed at the Sea View Apartments and this is where the first sign of Ben's street credibility came into play. At the time, Harry Enfield portraying Kevin and Perry on TV was popular, and we could understand just how the parents of these characters must have felt.

Thankfully it only lasted a day or so before he partnered me in games of table tennis, pool and darts, bringing back the good old days in our garage at home. It was after one of our games that Ben got talking to a guy of similar age who had been watching us play. Five minutes later, in the middle of their conversation, I got my cue to go. "See you later then, dad." OK mate, I know when I'm not wanted anymore.

The two soon became four and although we saw them around the hotel and pool area in the day, most evenings they would head off into the popular town, which for the guys was probably the best part of their holiday.

We did, however, impose a time curfew, which was met with a moan but usually respected. It was in the early hours of the morning and it was certainly no secret when he was back. After a kerfuffle, the bathroom and bedroom doors would finally be shut and, at last, it was lights out.

After a couple of friendly games, the season was finally under way. Parkway Tavern FC boasted a first and reserve team, much to the delight of many new players. Ben was selected for the first team, along with mates Jamie White and Andrew Jones. As expected, Lawrence Benson also lined up, so now they were both in the same team.

It only took a few games before the pair started to form an easygoing, friendly relationship. Lawrence played in defence with Ben further in front of him, sometimes on the wing, and they both started to link up well.

Lawrence says: "I could see that Ben was talented. He had superb balance, quick acceleration, an uncanny ability to keep hold of the ball and, of course, an eye for goal."

Off the pitch their friendship started to grow stronger. In fact, Ben renamed his new friend Lorenzo Pinamonte. The name stuck.

Ben's circle of friends at the Parkway Tavern had now increased significantly. Along with his girl group, other young ladies and guys were starting to visit regularly, creating a new group as well as a really friendly atmosphere. They also helped to aid his love of gambling on the fruit machine. His new friends would stand in front of the machine forming a human shield to disguise his playing from the watchful eyes of Mike and Sandy. Winnings were usually fed back into the machine, although not all – some had to be saved for an extra packet of crisps. After all, he had now gained the reputation of being a connoisseur when eating them.

Finding success was becoming hard for Parkway Tavern FC. Both teams were comprised of mainly local youths who had gravitated to the club to get a game on Saturday afternoons. Some of the lads had lots of raw talent but as a team they never had a clue how to win games against older, more experienced teams. The club always existed in the shadow of Stoke Gifford FC.

Lorenzo, like Ben, shared a passion for Bristol Rovers so, along with Jamie and Andy, they took a taxi over to Ashton Gate to watch the Bristol derby. It ended up being quite a painful experience, not only losing 3-2 to City but to rub salt into the wound the police formed a human barrier blocking the exit for away fans at the end of the game. This allowed the home fans to leave the ground first, but not before many were hurling abuse and humiliating their opposite number, who in turn vented their anger and frustration at the police. But not all of them. Ben had found something else to entertain him in the shape of an attractive female police officer. OK, maybe he needed to do some work on his chat up lines, but it certainly lightened the mood and provided some fun, at least for the four of them.

As the season concluded, Parkway Tavern Reserves achieved the unenviable status of being rated as the worst team in the country, finishing bottom of the table with an atrocious goals against record. However, this did provide the chance of a BBC appearance on the programme *Do Us A Favour*, which was hosted by Carol Smillie, along with Ralph Little of *The Royle Family* fame. The aim of the show was to provide Parkway's young keeper Luke Preddy with some expert coaching from none other than former England and Arsenal keeper David Seaman. Although they played in the first team, this was too good an opportunity for Ben and Lorenzo to miss, so the pair tagged along to the studios to witness the filming. It did not live up to expectations. The live part of the show was taken from the *Blue Peter* garden, where Seaman offered Luke some meaningless expert advice. The real fun began off air. While others were harassing him for autographs, Ben was asking him why he had such a ridiculous pony tail. He even had the audacity to reach up and tug it. "The missus likes it," muttered Seaman in a gruff northern accent, clearly not enamoured by Ben's forwardness. Yet as a Tottenham fan, this was classed as a minor victory over the Gunners legend.

Next on the hit list was Claire from the pop group Steps, who had just performed live on the show. As the lads were making their way back to their own dressing room, she was outside hers talking on her mobile phone. Ben tapped her on the shoulder and with a cheeky smile said: "Alright love?" She turned her head to meet Ben's gaze with a scowl of disgust, which made him laugh. After all, here he was in his element bringing these stars down a peg or two as they marched their way through the BBC building.

Shortly after turning 17, Ben learned that he would have to be mindful of his cheekiness to others, especially after having an altercation with an older player during pre-season training at Mead Park. He was now staking his claim to play as an out-and-out striker. Since he was a young boy, this had been his favoured position and now he was determined to prove it was his best.

One evening he was sharing some banter with his team-mate Dave, who was finding it hard to win the ball from Ben. In fact, each failed attempt to prise it away only served to fuel Dave's frustration. Eventually he became far more aggressive and his sliding tackles were being launched to cause injury rather than win the ball. As for Ben, for each lunge he evaded, his tongue became a tad sharper. Dave eventually threw a punch, which fortunately missed, but the training game stopped as everyone gawked at the two team-mates. Luckily, Ben escaped unscathed and soon after Dave left the club, never to be seen again. But this had been a lesson for Ben to learn – in the future maybe he would have to choose his victims more carefully.

Saturday, September 1 was an exciting day as we arrived in Palma Nova, Majorca and checked into the Rose Del Mar Apartments before rushing out to find a bar with a large screen TV. This year we had already agreed for Ben to bring Andrew Jones with him for company, but unfortunately he had to cancel at the last minute so a late replacement was found in the shape of "Bubble", a nickname he had gained from the TV programme *Big Brother*.

We found a bar with outside tables and chairs right by the water's edge, so we ordered our drinks and prepared to watch Germany v England in an important World Cup qualifier. The game had barely started when Germany went a goal up – great! Then our luck changed. Not only did we equalise, we went on to win 5-1. What a lovely start to the holiday!

After many celebrations, Gloria and I started to make our way back to the apartments – although in the dark we didn't actually have a clue where they were. After walking for ages, I eventually flagged down a taxi and we both jumped in, glad to finally be resting our legs. I said to the driver: "The Rose Del Mar Apartments, please mate." At which he then just pointed his finger to the other side of the road. Oh no! With bright red faces, Gloria and I got out and crossed the road to our accommodation.

During our stay, the guys just did not get on. Bubble usually went back to the apartment alone and insisted on having the light on in their room so he could read. Ben objected to this so spent most nights sleeping on the balcony. He did, however, befriend a bunch of Geordie lads who had a lot more in common with him. Most evenings they could be found in a popular music bar singing and dancing. Their holiday anthem song was undoubtedly *Hey Baby!* By DJ Ötzi. They all danced on the chairs and tables to this one.

During the daytime, episodes of Ben's favourite comedy programme were shown on many TVs around the bars. *Only Fools And Horses* also proved popular with the Geordie lads.

There was disturbing news on September 11 when there were co-ordinated terrorist attacks on the twin towers in Manhattan. At the end of our holiday I think one of the guys was happy to be returning home, in his own way of course.

Finding a career was not getting easier for Ben so to help funds, he started working for one of the Tavern regulars. Steve Westlake (alias Wetleg) was digging up the roads in Swindon so Ben agreed to join him. He enjoyed the manual, outdoor job, which included loud music from the radio and plenty of ribbing from the other guys, which all added fun to the working day.

This was all made possible thanks to his Tavern connections, which had by now grown hugely. Even at such a young age, Ben knew almost everyone in the pub by name. His ability to find common ground with people from all walks of life was admirable, and often formed out of friendly banter. His musical taste, however, was becoming questionable - especially his love of cheesy tunes. Along with Gemma, it ensured the jukebox would normally be blasting out classics from Meatloaf, Spandau Ballet or maybe Culture Club. Well, at least they enjoyed it!

With the new season well under way, not only had Ben started up front but he was scoring goals on a regular basis. The first team at Parkway were enjoying a successful cup run and for the first time were feeling optimistic about their chances.

Gloria and I were given an early Christmas present when, on December 1, Mark announced the arrival of daughter Caitlin. The next day we were both Nottingham-bound, excited to see our first grandchild.

Andrew Jones (Joner) came round to stay and share our Christmas evening that year, arriving just in time for some festive fun and games.

Ben's two nans were also with us and they both took an instant liking to Joner, especially after Ben had told them a yarn or two about his past exploits – which they not only believed but were very impressed with.

The lucky nans won a bottle of their favourite tipple after winning Bingo games we all played together – and although our blunt pencils may have helped, it was worth it just to see their excited faces. They also enjoyed opening the stockings which Santa had left, revealing the usual chocolates and other goodies, although they stared in disbelief as the guys unwrapped theirs.

Out came more goodies, along with an inflatable sheep and doll, which gave the lads a laugh – although not as loud as the laugh from all of us after hearing one nan say to the other: "Don't you think they are a bit old for those now?"

The evening ended with our CD and tape player playing all the old songs, which the pair loved to sing along to.

Ben gained the first of many nicknames in the Parkway Tavern, much to the amusement of his mates. His cheekiness certainly never faded, that was one of his endearing qualities. Even so, he had to choose his victims carefully. One particular afternoon, a guy called Beaky got into a heated argument at the bar, which led to him receiving a huge punch to the side of his face. He then offered the other guy outside, where he well and truly finished off what had been started.

A few weeks later, Ben was sitting in the bar with his mates when Beaky came over to talk to him, squeezing himself onto the bench, which meant the others had to shuffle along to allow him space. He then firmly placed his arm around Ben's shoulder before talking quietly. The only words that were plain to hear were Ben saying: "Yes Beaky. No Beaky." Ten minutes later, Beaky picked up his things and left, at which point Ben declared that he needed to change his cacks! This left his mates in stitches of laughter and Ben with a new nickname.

Against all the odds, Parkway Tavern FC had made it to the final of the cup and Cacks had been scoring goals for fun. Then as the game approached, so was Ben – with an offer he found hard to resist. Stoke Gifford FC manager Paul Cooper asked him to join his team. Gifford had just lost their main goalscorer Paul Evans and were on the lookout for a striker. After careful thought, Ben decided to give it a go. He was curious to see not only if he could play at that level, but also if he could succeed.

By now, work had dried up with "Wetleg" so Ben decided to assist me with my complete bathrooms installation business. This gave him the chance to see the different trades involved in the work from start to finish while being in my customers' homes. It would maybe enable him to find a trade suitable to pursue as a career.

Ben hit the ground running for Stoke Gifford, scoring many crucial goals which boosted his confidence big time. Goals are important for any striker, but scoring goals in the Suburban Premier League's top division at the tender age of 17 was testament to just how talented he was. Yet despite this there was never any shred of arrogance shown.

Unfortunately, Bristol Parkway FC lost in the cup final – but worse was to follow when the club folded. This prompted Stoke Gifford FC to set up a third team, which many of the players joined. However, some of the Gifford players were not impressed. One senior player commented that he did not know how merging with the worst team in the country was ever going to make Stoke Gifford a better team. On the positive side, it did keep many of the local lads together as well as bringing some youth to the Gifford ranks.

When June 20 came round, there was a nice surprise for Ben. When he called into the Tavern in the evening, many of the locals – knowing it was his 18th birthday – had already lined up numerous pints of beer on the bar ready for his arrival. Shortly after, even Mike and

Sandy both gave him a hug and welcomed him to raise a glass, now it was legal. Later, with a broad smile, he took the opportunity to go around the tables and thank everyone for their welcome, only nowadays he didn't collect and return the empty glasses. However, it did provide him with the chance – like so many times before – to share a bit of banter before getting back down to the business of trying to sink some of the ales he's been bought.

An Addition To The Family

Ben really wanted Lorenzo to join him at Stoke Gifford. He was aware of his capabilities and believed he could also make the step up. So having got to know Lorenzo's parents, he set about using his charm and wit to encourage his mum to provide some added persuasion for him to make the move. It certainly worked and when Lorenzo did accept, they were the only two players taken into the first team from Bristol Parkway FC. How times had changed, when they first met Lorenzo considered Ben to be a footballing rival. Now, less than two years later, they were best mates looking to play together at a good level. The pair did take a while to get to know the Gifford lads, who took their football very seriously. They didn't like losing, although it was something the new pair has been accustomed to. Nevertheless, they both got their heads down and got stuck in as the season started, both determined to prove their worth.

When Gifford signed Ben as a young striker with huge potential, little did they know the package they were inheriting. The club would soon be entering a new era and things would be very different.

Gloria and I took our first holiday away on our own that year. We flew off to Portugal to stay in an apartment in Albufeira for a week – and what an experience it was. I nearly got arrested for being a thief! One morning we were out shopping along the main strip, which had lots of market stalls selling a variety of items. This offered Gloria the chance, true to form, to spot endless bargains. She purchased so many that I ended up following on behind her with a full bag on each arm.

Suddenly, a young Portuguese lady called me over to look at some gold jewellery she was selling. Not to appear rude, I walked over and then she insisted I should try one of the items on. In a polite manner, I said: "Thanks, but no thanks." She then ran from behind her stall and placed a gold chain around my neck, assuring me it looked beautiful and suited me. I called out to Gloria, who came over to see what was going on. In an instant she told me to take it off, but as both my hands were holding the bags I asked if she would do it.

Suddenly the lady got angry and started shouting at me, demanding that I should pay for the chain. It got even worse when she pointed at me and kept shouting: "Thief! Thief!" – especially as two police officers, with guns in their holsters, were passing at the time and looked over in our direction, which worried me. Gloria reacted quickly and grabbed the chain from my neck and returned it to the lady, although she was reluctant to take it back. Only when the police officers walked away did she take it back, but not without a scowl of disgust. Gloria assured me the chain was not a bargain – which was good enough for me as I never wanted one anyway!

Meanwhile, back at home, little did we know of a new trend that was about to start every time we took a holiday at home or abroad. The house suddenly became a disco, a nightclub, a venue for guests to come and party the night away. Personnel would be expected to treat the house with respect, but for the chosen ones fun and laughter was guaranteed.

At the Tavern, Ben started to form a comical relationship with a guy who was 50 years his senior. It must be said that Mike Berry was a heavy drinker who liked having a chat, and Ben did have a way of extracting the most elaborate and obscure stories imaginable. Even so, to this day I still doubt that when playing football he once scored a penalty with his head or that he once jumped up to swing on the hoop when playing basketball for Great Britain. The tales, however, did provide a giggle for all around so Ben encouraged Mike, who had a wonderful gift for embellishing the simplest of stories once he had an ear to listen to him.

Unknown to Ben, I went along to witness a few home games at Gifford to see how he was progressing and from what I saw I certainly felt he was ready to do himself justice as a striker to fear. In terms of height, he was a late developer. It was only in his late teens that he actually gained height as well as body strength. Now he had all the attributes he lacked in previous years. I felt now was the time for him to train with a semi-professional or even a professional club, but mentioning this just brought a smile to his face and the simple reply: "I don't think so dad."

Practical working at a hands-on level was not really appealing to Ben, so he stopped working with me and started a new job carrying out general duties at Bristol Parkway railway station. It was here he met Adam, a guy he soon took pity on – especially as the poor young man had been told to leave home and had nowhere else to live. Following Ben's pleading, Adam came to live with us, sharing Ben's room while he looked for other options. He also shared Ben's clothes, trainers and food, which certainly helped him save money towards his next accommodation. We all developed affection for Adam, who seemed a really nice young man, so as the weeks passed, he became part of our family.

Gloria, Rachel and I took a nice break to Gran Canaria for a week, leaving the guys with smiles and hugs, although our faces were the complete opposite on our return home to an empty house. It appeared as though a bomb had hit the place. Utensils, pans and crockery being left everywhere in the kitchen was fine, but all the other rooms were in a complete shambles. Probably the worst was the bedroom, where Gloria had to make her way through clothes strewn everywhere across the floor. She was absolutely fuming so it was no surprise that when the guys returned home from work, Adam was instantly shown the red card and ordered to leave.

For the second year running, Ben finished as top scorer – albeit this time for Stoke Gifford, who ended the season in 12th position with both new guys slowly settling into the team and feeling more at ease with their new team-mates. A new sense of humour was also being introduced. The Speakeasy Room was suddenly becoming a far funnier place to be, as were the shower and changing rooms. The Speakeasy was a large room in the Poplar Rooms building based at Gifford's home ground on North Road.

Saturdays would see all three teams meet up in the room after playing, which enabled all of them to get to know each other on a social basis. There is where the fun got started for many of the Gifford lads. They adored Ben's youthful cheekiness. He was like a breath of fresh air with his sense of humour and mad antics. Suddenly the atmosphere was warm, welcoming and full of fun. Even the more senior players were reacting with a smile or two, regardless of the day's result.

Ben's time working at Parkway station was cut relatively short following an application and interview which saw him get a new job. This was an opportunity to move forward so he consequently started work in the call centre of the Royal Bank of Scotland, based near the centre of Bristol.

Shortly after he started, Gloria and I received an interesting letter from a lady in Weston-super-Mare. It turned out to be from Adam's mum, who had only recently learned of his prolonged stay with us. She was very apologetic and grateful for the way her son had been treated and apparently this was not the first episode of this kind. She even offered to reimburse us for the costs of his stay, but we were happy that she took the time to make us aware so we replied with thanks and wished her well for the future.

An unexpected visitor from a far off land turned up at training at Gifford one evening. He was a Chinese gentleman whose English name was Dave. He came to enquire about joining the ranks at the club as he was on a work placement and staying in North Road, although he could barely speak a word of English. Ben took an instant liking to the young man and immediately gave him the nickname Miyagi. His enthusiasm was infectious and he was the nicest of blokes.

To help with his English, Dave carried an electronic translator, which Ben abused purely for amusement. He often entered crude words in place of those Dave was actually looking for, chuckling away as Dave looked at the translation bemused and confused. Ben did try to get Miyagi involved in everything and he became something of a mascot at Gifford. Ben regularly took him to the Tavern as well as the Memorial Stadium to watch Rovers. He even tried to teach him the words to *Goodnight Irene.*

One Saturday, Dave was asked to be a linesman for a game at Gifford. Whenever the opposition were through on goal, Ben would only have to shout for offside and the flag would go up, much to the anger of the opposition! He was like Ben's puppet but it was comedy gold.

Another Saturday evening, Ben took Dave to meet up with other mates at a bar in town where he decided to give Miyagi a taste of cider. After half a pint, Dave's face was planted firmly down on the table and the only time he stirred was when Ben proposed a toast – but even then he could only raise his glass to within a whisker of his lips before his head crashed back down on the table again, which caused fits of laughter from the others. But Dave was always well looked after by Ben and the other lads so it was a sad day when he had to return home but not before a strong embrace from Ben and plenty of smiles to send him on his way.

Chapter Nine

SHOWER AND DRESSING ROOM FUN

Some bad news came about when it was announced the Parkway Tavern was to close. For many it was the centre of the Gifford community, a place full of banter where everyone knew everybody else. The pub was going to be refurbished and turned into a modern bar with new management and renamed The Parkway. The brewery's aim was to make it more aesthetically pleasing in the hope of attracting new customers and not just the Gifford locals, so it was destined to lose its community feel. It saw regulars moving around the corner to frequent the Beaufort Arms. With the sudden additional influx of customers, their bar tills were soon ringing loudly.

It was in the Beaufort Ben became even more acquainted with his Gifford team-mate Neil Whalen, along with his two children Reece and Ellie. Neil had previously played at an even higher level of football with Bristol Manor Farm, but like many others returned to the club he loved.

The three of them loved Ben's personality and infectious smile and it soon became a common sight, when Ben wasn't keeping the fruit machine busy, that he would be out on the green across the road playing

84

with Reece and Ellie. They enjoyed each other's company so much he often ended up going back to their home to play computer games, which included a sleepover. He was always made welcome in the Whalen household.

Partway through the season, Gifford welcomed two new additions to the squad. Jamie West (Westy) already knew Ben from their Tavern days so now their friendship would grow even more. Match days would usually see the pair meet up at the Beaufort for soft drinks before going to the ground. James Stephens, a year younger than Ben, was a character in his own right. The pair had much in common – including their sense of humour – so it wasn't long before James was renamed Garth!

The Parkway conveniently reopened just in time for the Rugby World Cup, which was taking place in Australia. The one advantage it had over the Beaufort was that it screened live sports events. This did attract some of the younger originals back, although with the time difference in Australia it was usually at the crack of dawn. So for Ben, Lorenzo, Gemma and others, late-night drinking was often backed up by a "hair of the dog" the following morning. It was well worth it though when Jonny Wilkinson and the rest of the England boys won the competition.

Although Ben finished top scorer at the end of the season, Gifford had only just escaped relegation. But on the fun side, two new traditions had commenced at the Poplar Rooms.

A portable CD player was now placed in the changing room before games, blasting out cheesy classics in an effort to create an upbeat atmosphere. The newer brigade especially loved it. Post-match in the shower and changing room was also becoming more interesting. Ben would encourage others having a shower to join him belting out the chorus of a classic song. His practical jokes were also evident. It might be just the tame squeezing of shower gel onto a mate's head or the good old-fashioned wet towel whipping. Of course, the size of one's manhood would never go unnoticed – there was no hiding place. So unless you were Big Tom, notoriety might come your way for the wrong reasons.

The best, though, was usually saved for the last guy in the showers, who suddenly found the changing room door locked. This meant to get back in he would have to walk outside and venture around the building before re-entering through The Speakeasy Room door with only a towel to cover up the crown jewels. A rousing reception was always waiting, especially after the towel was tugged away!

June 17 had been a long, hard day at work for me so I was happy to be finally heading home. On the way I had to call into the local B&Q store, which was due to close at 8pm, to pick up some materials for the following day. With time running out, I hastily approached Stoke Gifford, but suddenly traffic came to a halt not far from the new Parkway pub. I waited for a while, which was frustrating as the store was only two minutes away. Then, to my anger and astonishment, I could see and hear football fans singing and dancing. England had just beaten Switzerland in the European Championships with a young Wayne Rooney scoring a goal.

I was not happy though. My fist was raised ready to vent my anger and frustration at these hooligans, who were in a long line doing the conga dance whilst smiling, waving and weaving in and out of the stationary vehicles. Some of them even had the audacity to tap on the windscreens before cheering out loud.

As they approached my van, I stared in disbelief. OMG no, it can't be... but oh yes it was. Ben was the leader of the conga. When he realised it was me in the van, he smiled, waved and shouted his usual greeting: "Alright dad, how ya doing?" I was gobsmacked. Without even realising it, my fist had turned into a wave, my thumb had planted itself behind my index finger as I waved from my wrist, a bit like how the Queen waves to the public from her car. My face had a bemused smile as I sat stunned. After a while they passed by so the traffic finally started moving – and I managed to make it to the store with a minute to spare.

Like many others, Mike Berry was now frequenting the Beaufort on a regular basis. But with the greatest respect, there were times Ben was keen to avoid him. Mike could quite easily make a single, passing comment last for over a month once he had your ear, so any plans for the evening had to be cancelled. Knowing this, Hiscox had an amazing way of greeting Mike before craftily befriending and passing him off to a mate of his choice who would then be stuck with him for the rest of the night.

Like many others, Ben Manns had been a victim before. Yet it was all about to change when Mike let it be known one night he had a long lost nephew from Devon he believed had moved to Bristol. Upon hearing this, Hiscox decided it would be hilarious to convince Mike that Manns was indeed the relative in question. He had conversations with Mike over a period of weeks before building up a picture of the nephew. He then cunningly used all the details he had built up to convince Mike than Manns was indeed the man – and somehow it worked! From that day forward, Manns was the first person Mike went over to as soon as he entered the pub – and last given how long he spoke for.

Hiscox, of course, found it utterly hilarious – Manns far less so after the first five hours.

The following season at Gifford saw another tradition put in place with Hiscox having an accomplice at every game. It came in the shape of a large silver radio which would always be placed pitch side as the game started, then as soon as it finished it would be placed on his shoulder close to his ear. This enabled him to hear all the day's final scores as they came in, Rovers and Tottenham of course the priorities. These, along with Gifford's result, would determine whether it had been a good day at the office or not.

The popular shower song he had all the lads singing along to was Marvin Gaye's classic *Sexual Healing*. The club's treasurer, who was called Dave Pealing, became the unlucky man who had his name included in the revised version of the song. So when the chorus came along, the original was replaced with the new version and went: "When I get that feeling, I want sex with Dave Pealing." It was belted out by all. For many lads these words will always remain as part of the song. However, the season ended on a disappointing note as Gifford were relegated to Division Two.

The location of Ben's job and time-consuming trips to get there and back were beginning to take their toll on Ben so shortly after his 21st birthday, he started a new job at Integral, a company based fairly locally at Aztec West. His role as customer service co-ordinator included arranging different tradesmen to carry out maintenance works for various clients. He soon got to know more about many of the guys and shared some jokes and banter with them. But the banter did not go down too well initially in the office he shared with Cherilyn Preece, who had recently returned after maternity leave. The manager even decided to split them up, although this did not stop the brotherly-sisterly relationship they had formed. On the quiet, he often popped in to see her, often armed with some squares of chocolate and a coffee, which they both shared over the computer along with a chat, all the while keeping their heads firmly down.

A typical Saturday night out in town would often see Ben disappear from his group of mates, although he could usually be found on the dancefloor with a bottle of blue WKD in his hand, pulling out the moves to the music he loved.

Lorenzo explains: "A night out for Ben wasn't really about pulling a bird, it was about letting himself go, having a good time and a laugh with his mates whilst sharing some banter with the girls he'd just met. He just wanted to dance to the cheesiest music with someone old enough to be his grandmother! At the end of the night he gained a lot of joy seeing the horrific messes that some of our mates would end up pulling and the drunken states they would get themselves in.

"He didn't require alcohol to enjoy himself and have a good time. For example, he could quite easily walk into the Beaufort with a few quid in his pocket and still have a good night."

The fruit machine, though, rarely escaped his attention.

*Who The ******* Hell Is Dennis?*

Two new players joined up with Gifford ready for the start of the new season. Carl Rutter (Rutts) and Dan Dunt (Dunty) provided more ammunition which could hopefully fire the team straight back into Division One.

Sunday football also came into play this year when Merryweather Old Boys started out, consisting mainly of a mixture of guys from all three Gifford teams. This was a big ask as the kick-off time was 10.30am so an early night was advised to all the lads involved. Some hope!

One rare Saturday saw Ben Manns sat in the Beaufort without the attention of Mike Berry but with the company of Hiscox and another mate. He was trying to work out the cost of something whilst doing the calculation out loud. In a ridiculously short amount of time, Hiscox shouted out the answer – which Manns completely ignored, believing it to be a wind-up. After struggling for a few minutes, he eventually gave up and used the calculator on his phone. Then he came to realise that Hiscox had, in fact, been correct. Not willing to let this lie, he asked Hiscox how he had managed to calculate the answer so quickly. Hiscox replied he could calculate any mathematical equation with ease. This brought laughter from Manns and his mate, only for Hiscox to retort: "No, seriously!"

Over the next 20 minutes or so, they took turns to throw ridiculously difficult mathematical calculations at Hiscox, all of which received a pretty much instant reply. After using a calculator to check, they realised he had given the correct answers. Standing back in amazement, Manns' analysis was simple: "Hiscox is definitely a smoking, blue WKD-drinking – Stephen Hawking!"

Things were looking good for Gifford, who were perched on top of the table with Hiscox top scoring once again. He was about to be joined by a 16-year-old striker. Luke Bartley had started out in the third team when the season started, but his talent earned him promotion to the first team, where he was welcomed by all.

Luke says: "Everyone welcomed me but Ben made an extra effort. He was the biggest character in the changing room and, trust me, there were a few. He was always joking around taking the mick out of everyone, including himself. He had no ego at all – that's why everyone loved him."

Luke was given the nickname Barts and his addition was an influence on Gifford, who finished top to gain promotion back to Premier Division One at the first attempt.

Call it childlike humour or the actions of a wind-up merchant but Ben loved to set his victims up. He was gaining a reputation for it but it provided many laughs. During one of his famous house parties one evening he called down to Gemma and asked if she could pop upstairs to help him in the bathroom. Happy to oblige, she went up and walked in before screaming out loud. There was "Stinky Turner" having a bath. She never even offered to scrub his back!.

One evening in the Parkway, a few of the lads were in checking out the new barmaid when Ben decided to prod James Hindle in the back, who then naturally turned around to see who was responsible. Following repeated prodding, Hindle kept on glancing round and eventually it was wearing pretty thin until he assumed he'd found the culprit. He then quickly turned around and landed a swift slap across the chops of Lorenzo, who had been innocently talking to another mate. One person who did find it hilarious though was the new barmaid, 18-year-old Zoe Matthews. She had only just become aware of Ben and the others after starting her new job.

With the new season well under way for Gifford, there was good and bad news. On the bright side, two 18-year-old lads Dave Talbot and Ross Matthews joined to boost the first team. But Lorenzo's season was looking doubtful because of injury.

Ben was playing at the top of his game and after another man-of-the-match performance during an important game, manager Martin Black was contacted by the local press to provide details of the game. Perhaps the phone line was poor – or maybe it was Martin's Bristolian accent – but the report which appeared in the *Bristol Evening Post* was headlined: "Two goals from Dennis Cox secures victory for Gifford."

So Ben Hiscox became Dennis Cox and another nickname was gained. Without doubt, this was to be the most famous of them all and the lads loved it. From that day on, they all referred to him as Dennis with affection. In fact, from that day on, all future press reports covering his football exploits also referred to him as Dennis Cox, so it soon became a regular name in the printed headlines.

Ben's presence was also having an effect on some of his work colleagues at Integral, especially two young ladies. Elle Llewellyn commented: He never fails to get a smile from anyone he speaks to. In my mind, he's a mischief maker with a heart of gold."

Sharon Gibbs added: "Some of the things he comes out with are so funny. The innuendos are becoming legendary in our office."

Sharon and her family are all Bristol City fans and her children especially love the banter that goes on between them. She said: "When my kids come to meet me at work the first thing they ask is whether Ben is working. Sometimes I think they look forward more to seeing him than to me!" The fun certainly helped to make the workplace a happier one with the days passing by with a smile.

Bristol Rovers got through to the final of the Johnstone's Paint Trophy, which was to be played at the Millennium Stadium in Cardiff, after beating arch-rivals City in a two-legged semi-final. Ben made a weekend of it in Cardiff staying in a hostel and bed sharing with Lorenzo, Jamie and Joner. Let's hope the window was fully open. While out and about during the evening they got to meet up and have some fun with Jon Tickle of *Big Brother* fame. The final itself was against Doncaster Rovers and was deadlocked at 2-2 after 90 minutes before the Yorkshire club went on to win 3-2 after extra time.

Stoke Gifford ended their season back in Division One in a respectable seventh spot, with Dennis top scoring again. His favourite song he had all the lads singing in the showers was Culture Club's classic *Karma Chameleon*. He'd text them all the words in the week so the choir was well prepared.

Rovers were given the chance to play at the new Wembley Stadium after making it through to the League two play-off final against Shrewsbury Town. The winners would gain promotion. True friendship came to light when staunch City fan Neil Whalen drove a minibus to London for Ben and many others from the Beaufort to watch the game. Just three minutes in, Neil was laughing and mocking the lads when Shrewsbury went a goal up. But Rovers then equalised and went in at the interval 2-1 up. With virtually the last kick of the game, they scored again to secure a 3-1 win. Euphoria and ecstasy peaked at that point and poor Neil found himself at the very bottom of a pile of lads who had pounced on him during their celebrations. The journey home was fun filled with singing and dancing on the bus. The Kaiser Chiefs' hit *Ruby* became the theme song of the day. It was a great day with great fun had by all – bar one. The one who had helped to make the day such a memorable one, mainly for all the others..

Numbers were increasing alarmingly at the Hiscox house parties, which were always guaranteed to be a great night. However, it got to a point where just too many were turning up so the situation needed addressing. In his wisdom and to save grace, Ben cunningly appointed Gemma and Hannah to act as door stewards to turn uninvited visitors away, which they did – but only after sarcastically whispering into his ear: "Wimp!"

The house was usually treated with the utmost respect by all who attended so damage was limited, although Ben did have one major worry. Gloria's treasured possessions in the garden were her gnomes, so the golden rule spelled out in repeated requests was that these were not to be touched. This, of course, was a big mistake as everybody who came would make it their major goal to move as many as possible. Suddenly, gnomes were being hidden everywhere inside the house and in the garden. When he realised what was happening, the expression on Ben's face became one of pure panic. On the positive side, none of the gnomes were broken. But on the negative side, he now had to try and remember exactly which gnome belonged where.

Meanwhile Rachel, who was training to become a police constable, had been dating a local guy for quite a while and things were looking to become quite serious. Michael Bird appeared on the scene and our first impressions were that he was a really nice young man – although there was a hillbilly element about him with his long hair and whiskers. My initial fears of Ben ribbing him about his appearance were thankfully unwarranted. After introduction, they both exchanged humour and polite conversation. Maybe it was out of respect for his sister that there was no banter involved. Or not yet, anyway.

The Merryweather Sunday football regime was well under way, which meant that our home was becoming like a fully booked hotel. It was interesting in the mornings meeting the various new faces who had arrived the previous night, usually the worse for wear. We soon got to know quite a few different individuals who, to be fair, were always polite and gracious. But their state of tiredness and speech suggested the alcohol level in their bodies was still very high. It was astounding to think they were going off to play football.

Of all the regulars, two were pretty much certainties. Ben Bennett and James Stephens (Garth) were looking to become season ticket-holders at our Sunday morning club. Gloria and I got to know them even better as they always provided humorous conversations, so it soon became evident they were fun guys, although we did not expect their acquaintance in the middle of the night. We assumed they must be naturists as, after a visit to the loo, one of them often entered our bedroom by mistake – sometimes wearing boxers but more often not. We soon got to recognise their faces too!

Injuries had by now taken their toll on Lorenzo, who when available was mainly consigned to the reserves for the season ahead. Generally, the first-team squad at Gifford were a younger age level, with many of the new guys looking to gain the necessary experience to help the team achieve much-needed success.

There was a new kid in town at the Beaufort in the shape of a young lady who was simply stunning. All the guys had noticed and admired her so it was no surprise one evening when one of them decided he fancied his chances. Ben Manns had been keeping an eye out and after sinking a few beers, he was contemplating making a move. So with his usual ever-trusting instinct he foolishly confided in his mate Hiscox, who reassured him and convinced him to go for it, mainly because it gave him the chance to play the old game "Johnny" to see if he could catch him out.

The game was simple – go to the gents' toilet and buy a packet of condoms, remove one from the wrapper and then attempt to place it on your mate's shoulder without them realising. So with a bit of Dutch courage and a huge shove from Hiscox, Manns decided to go over and try his luck. To his surprise, he got chatting and actually hit it off quite well. Her reaction was both welcoming and pleasant. She appeared to be very easygoing. Then, about 10 minutes into their conversation, the young lady was in stitches laughing at everything that came out of Manns' mouth. He was beginning to think he should be in stand-up comedy since half of what he was saying was not even remotely funny.

Midway through his next sentence he faintly heard a voice from behind saying: "Hey Johnny!" And with that, his heart sank. He knew that was the code for letting people know that the johnny was in play. Putting two and two together, he glanced down at his left shoulder and yes, there it was. So it wasn't his wonderful wit that was charming her after all. There was more evidence of that when he turned his head back up to discover that the young lady had gone and was nowhere to be seen. He did, however, see a smiling face at the bar. That of Mr Hiscox.

Later that evening on his customary tour of the pub, Hiscox noticed a young lady sat on her own, so he went over to join her. Zoe Matthews then provided plenty of baby talk as she was nearing the end of her pregnancy and was excited about the forthcoming birth. He shared the conversation with interest for a while before swiftly returning to the bar for a refill.

Gifford again ended the season in seventh position with their young side improving all the while. But word had spread around the camp that Martin's brother John Black had accepted the job as manager of Bristol Manor Farm and had offered Ben and a few others the chance to join him.

Manor Farm play in the Premier Division of the Toolstation Western League, so this would involve a fair amount of travelling. Ben was undecided about the move, mainly because of the loyal friendships he had made with all the lads at Gifford. His mind, though, was made up after advice from Neil Whalen, who was an admirer of Ben's balance, pace and eye for goal. He insisted that with those capabilities, Ben would do well at the higher level and at his age, now was the time to give it a shot. So along with a few of the other guys, he made the switch to join a new group of players, all hoping to form a team that could bring even more success to a highly respected club.

A new addition sat at the table with our family for Christmas dinner that year. Michael Bird was not only made welcome but mixed well with everyone. Gone was the long hair and caveman appearance to be replaced by extremely short hair and a fresh, clean look. Mark was an absentee that year although part of the way through our lunch, the phone rang and it was exciting news. He was calling from a hospital in Nottingham to say his partner Sarah had just given birth to his second daughter and they had named her Violet. He assured us mum and baby were doing fine, although he was totally exhausted!.

I made no comment about Mike's new appearance, yet I was pretty astonished. He's actually a decent-looking guy! Ben was sat opposite him and they were sharing a few laughs. I did notice Ben kept staring at him with a smile. Doubtless something was in the pipeline for future reference.

Having had a drink, Gloria was slightly emotional following the arrival of our second granddaughter. All plans for Boxing Day were now cancelled so we could pay a visit. Ben then had fun with his gran, testing her every 10 minutes on the name of the new-born. The alcohol though had affected her too. Not once could she remember the baby's correct name – although she found it hysterical trying to guess, even though she kept coming up with the wrong one. I had already planned our evening with some fun and entertainment – and it will be interesting to see how Mike reacts. Well, at least he's already let his hair down!

Ben was making a good impression on and off the pitch at Manor Farm. Along with defender Ben Murray, they were performing the classic Vinnie Jones and Paul Gascoigne act in training, with the defender's crown jewels being on the receiving end. The shower and dressing rooms were again very lively and in the clubhouse after training, they all enjoyed free food. The chef often came around with leftovers for whoever wanted more, but Ben's reply – "No thanks, I'm driving!" always brought laughs all round.

Career-wise, Ben now felt he wanted a new challenge and maybe a slightly different line of work, so he was excited yet nervous after passing his first interview at nearby Rolls-Royce. When he returned for the second interview, it could not have gone better and despite competition from many other applicants, he was offered the job and duly accepted it.

Two weeks later, he joined the workforce of engineering firm Mitie working as part of the first team at Rolls-Royce as a mechanical and electrical administrator. Only time would tell how successful he would be.

Manor Farm were progressing well in the league and the FA Vase, where the next round presented them with an away tie at Brighton side Peacehaven. During the journey to Sussex, Ben decided to ring manager John Black pretending to be a representative from the FA. He created a concoction of lies about problems with the pitch and warning of a possible postponement or a delayed kick-off time. Naturally, John was not a happy man – until he arrived at the ground and realised the phone call must have been a hoax. The other lads thought it was hilarious – especially as Ben was in the back and John in the front of the same vehicle at the time! The game went well for Manor Farm though with Ben scoring as they won the tie 3-0.

The journey back home was even more hilarious. John received a call from the FA asking for his views and comments on the game. Thinking it was another hoax, he spoke to the caller in no uncertain terms before hanging up. But after further communication the following day, he learned the call had actually been genuine and so he rang the FA to apologise.

At the end of the season, the lads had done him proud, not only in the Vase but by finishing fifth in the league, which was a major success for his new team. Ben ended his first season of Western League football as the club's top scorer and his familiar goal celebration – one arm in the air and one finger raised – was witnessed many times, much to the team's delight.

Chapter Ten

WEDDING BELLS CHIME!

One of the original group of Ben's friends, Gemma Walker, had tied the knot and was now to be known as Fisher, so Ben went along to the evening celebrations. Shortly after arriving, he went over to greet Gemma. But rather than stating the obvious, he told her: "Oh my god Gem, you look… disgusting!" Luckily, Gemma found it hilarious. "Typical!" she said. "The king of mickey-taking." After a laugh and a hug, the celebrations carried on well into the night.

There was, however, one occasion when Gemma did get upset by something Ben had said – and it was the only time she then saw him in a serious mood. "When Ben found out he had upset me, he was genuinely upset too," she said. "He made a real effort to make things right. He showed me then he really did care about my feelings." Afterwards, the issue became a minor one – it was never going to ruin their true friendship.

All the players at Stoke Gifford were excited about the new season. Finally, after many years of construction, the new clubhouse had finally been completed. It provided new changing and shower rooms as well as a large room with a kitchen and bar. This replaced the old Speakeasy Room and the Poplar Rooms building, which was no longer required.

The new clubhouse was located very close to the pitch, which enabled both teams to walk straight out onto the playing surface.

Manor Farm were starting to hit top form and preparing for their biggest game for many years. A good run in the FA Cup gave them a home tie against Basingstoke, managed by former top professional Frank Gray, brother of former Leeds United legend Eddie.

It proved a very close game and in the final minutes, with the score 2-2, Ben – who had already scored – broke through. His attempt beat the keeper but hit the post and rebounded to safety, which meant a replay at Basingstoke.

The return game was another close affair. Ben gave the home defenders plenty of problems and won the man of the match award. But right at the death, Basingstoke nicked a goal against the run of play to win 1-0.

Their manager had been very impressed with Ben's performances in both games and got talking with John Black, asking how much Ben was being paid and how much he might be looking for to go and play for Basingstoke. With a big grin on his face, John replied: "You don't want him – he's a menace! He might come to you if you offer him a free pint and a packet of fags." In the distance, Ben was standing at the bar with a few of his team-mates. He had a pint in one hand and a… yes, you've guessed it!

Against all the odds, Sunday morning football with Merryweather was continuing, so it was no surprise when we got our usual middle-of-the-night wake-up call as Garth stumbled into our room after a visit to the loo. Not fully awake or aware, Gloria asked quite loudly: "Clive?" Garth replied: "I'm not Clive." By now I had raised my head off the pillow just enough to see it was Garth – this time with his boxers on! "Wrong room, mate," I advised him, before returning my head to the pillow. With that he left, doubtless to try the next room available.

Garth's habit of choosing the wrong room continued in the morning after a wind-up from Ben. Gloria and I were downstairs when she decided to use our cloakroom loo. Ben had got up to use the upstairs loo, only to find Bennett had beaten him to it. So he then went downstairs to use the cloakroom loo, only to find his mum parked on it doing the crossword. At this point I should explain that Gloria never locks the door.

Ben being fully aware of this, he simply said on entry: "Morning mum" before returning upstairs. He noticed that Garth had just surfaced and tried the bathroom door, only to find it locked with Bennett doing overtime. So Ben then advised Garth that if he was desperate, the downstairs loo was available. With a thankful nod, Garth headed downstairs and on entry found Gloria, who was stuck on five down in the crossword. "Oh! Morning Glor," he said. Slowly, with a touch of embarrassment, she looked up and said: "Alright Stephens?" With that, he went off on one. "Well, not too bad thanks Glor. Did you see Rovers yesterday? Any good?" The conversation went on for a minute or so with Ben cracking up on the landing. He was at last joined by a curious Bennett, wondering what he had missed.

Another Red Card

The news from Stoke Gifford was not good. They had just been relegated back down to Division Two. Meanwhile, Manor Farm ended the season in seventh place with Ben again top scorer. John Black felt a summer break for the lads was well deserved, so he booked a holiday to Magaluf in Majorca.

Shortly before leaving, Ben and Garth called into John's home in the village, but he was not around. However, they were greeted by his wife Jackie's mum. Who put the kettle on ready for a chat. Later, Ben nipped upstairs to use the loo – but also raided the couple's wardrobe.

After arriving in Magaluf and checking into the hotel – which had a tennis court and swimming pool – Ben decided to set the tone for the holiday. So he invited the lads to a winner-stays-on game of tennis, but said that their on-court wear should be the same as his. There was a surprise when they arrived as Ben was naked, somehow managing to cover up his parts with what he called a "mangina". So when play started, it wasn't just tennis balls that were flying around. The court was soon surrounded by a large crowd who were in tears of laughter. It was definitely not a sight for sore eyes.

One evening, it was fancy dress time. Or at least it was for Ben and Garth, who showed up dressed as John and Jackie Black. Their imitation and verbal expressions had the lads in stitches and even the real pair found it amusing – although they were glad to get their clothes back at the end of the evening.

On the final evening, Ben headed off on his own. The lads later went searching for him down on the strip of bars and eventually passed one which was packed. There was Ben – topless – banging out a karaoke version of 2 Unlimited's *No Limits*. The vocals might have needed a little fine tuning but at least the song had a beat and lots of people were dancing. The lads soon joined in too.

The holiday was a success in that it had extended closer friendships among all who went on it.

Michael Bird's relationship with Rachel was also going from strength to strength, as it was with Ben – although Michael may have been regretting his new look, as Ben labelled it, along with his dress sense, as highly questionable amid some sarcastic laughter. It was also pointed out to him that his hair was receding at the temples, which prompted the nickname Baldy. It was all in good fun though and the pair of them shared a comic relationship. Ben always referred to him as "my mate Mikey" – though not to his face. Rachel had now left the police force and was helping Mike with the catering side of his business.

On November 22, Mark and Sarah celebrated the birth of their daughter Tess, making us proud grandparents of three. Gloria had previously made the trip up to theirs to take care of Violet and Caitlin, and I was to join them at the weekend to take my turn at grabbing a cuddle.

Some of the family had to leave early on Christmas Night this year, which meant they would miss the entertainment I had planned. The not so lucky ones remaining were Rachel, Mike, Ben and his girlfriend. After a general knowledge quiz, it was down to the more serious stuff. Out in the hallway were two sacks full of clothes, wigs and hats, all ready to be worn. It was boys versus girls with Gloria the judge while I acted as DJ and musical director.

First in and dressed accordingly, with music playing in the background, were the girls, who entered the room to Abba's *Mamma Mia*. The dance routine and singing were excellent – in tune and in rhythm – but would it be enough to impress Judge Len...err, sorry, Gloria!

Next in were the boys dressed in black suits, hats, ties and sunglasses, once again with music in the background. The singing, and particularly the dancing, had to be seen to be believed. They were all over the shop, but all credit to their energy levels. They had me sweating just watching them. But their rendition of the Blues Brothers was enough to swing Judge Gloria's vote in their favour. That was a shock.

The next hour or so saw all of us letting our hair down, leaving the room then returning wearing something ridiculous to have a dance. It was crazy but who cares? We were having fun.

Mike was becoming accustomed to our annual celebrations and joined in with much enthusiasm, as did Ben's girlfriend. It was interesting overhearing a conversation she had with Rachel while Ben and Mike were out in the kitchen getting vital refreshments for all of us. Rachel asked how their relationship was going. Her reply – that they enjoyed each other's company and the time they spent together – sounded good. She did add that when they went out, which was usually to the Beaufort, they would end up having only a drink or two all night because Ben would often be wandering around all the tables talking to Tom, Dick and Harry. I thought to myself: "Hmmm. This young lady sounds like she's singing from the same songsheet as others before her – but you never know!

Work commitments and niggling injuries were starting to restrict the amount of games Ben was playing for Manor Farm and this, along with the time-consuming travel, was beginning to affect his enjoyment. The team, however, had a few new additions to the squad and were holding their own as the season progressed.

The question whether the Hiscox Hotel was to remain open all hours was put in serious jeopardy following a wake-up in the early hours of a frosty Sunday morning. There was a kerfuffle on the landing, which woke both of us. I went out to investigate and learned Garth had been sick while Ben and Bennett were trying to coax him back into the bedroom to get his head down. Ben assured me they both had it under control and, as he clearly did not want to disturb his mum, I agreed to help clear up while the guys continued the debate about getting Garth back into the bedroom for some shut-eye.

Things didn't go quite to plan as the continued noise saw Gloria appear. It went from bad to worse when Garth clumsily brushed past her, forcing her to take backward steps to keep her balance and stay on her feet. Then, for only the second time ever, she produced the red card – this time for Garth. Ben's pleas were cast aside – even I protested that obstruction only warrants a yellow – but to no avail.

The temperature outside was minus three and poor Garth was only wearing his boxers, so I proposed a judicial hearing, but the judge was having none of it. The end to it all saw Gloria standing by the open front door watching Garth leaving as Ben threw his clothes down from the bedroom window. But even that was pointless as Garth just put his shoes on before trudging away into the distance. We did see him a few days later – with his clothes back on. After an apology and a hug, he was not only forgiven but his red card was rescinded. He was back in her good books!

Martin Black was kept fully aware about the state of play at Manor Farm. He often met up with Ben and the lads in the Beaufort for a chat and an update. With a nudge and a wink, he always made it clear to his ex-strike partner that he would always be welcome back at Stoke Gifford, but only when the time was right.

Manor Farm finished the season in a creditable seventh place despite a few injury setbacks, but the news was not so good for Merryweather Old Boys. The Sunday mornings were finally taking their toll on the lads and the team folded.

Saturday, September 17 was a proud family day as Rachel and Mike tied the knot. Wedding bells rang as the smiling couple walked arm-in-arm out of a packed church. Usher Ben was busy meeting and greeting guests at the church as well as the reception, his natural warmth and smile making him popular with everyone who attended.

In the evening, the dancefloor also proved popular and this is where his stamina came to the fore. From the beginning of the night to the end he remained there, dancing with numerous guests until they returned to their tables. At the end of the night his only accomplice was a bottle of blue WKD, which he held in one hand while he continued to boogie – until the bride and groom finally got to join him to see out the evening and a memorable day.

Martin Black's hopes of a return to Division One were given a boost when Hiscox and the boys returned to Gifford for the new season. Westy also came back so, along with the younger lads, it looked a good recipe for success. For those returning, this was the first chance to use the new clubhouse. But the most refreshing sight of all was that of Hiscox – and his radio – back where they belonged.

Shortly after Rachel's wedding, I noticed a definite change in Ben, which became more apparent as the days passed. We didn't see that much of him at home anyway, but when we did, he seemed less relaxed than normal. In confidence, he even asked about the possibility of getting a mortgage or maybe a loan with a view to renting, making it clear he wanted to leave home and move on in his life. I supported his wish and made it clear I would help any way I could. So after taking some advice, he opened a new savings account in an effort to make the move a reality. The way he started to boost it was evidence he was certainly serious.

The mixture of experience and youth was working wonders at Gifford, who were sitting on top of the division. Young Lewis Daniels had just made it into the first team having started out in the third team aged 15, when he had first become aware of Hiscox. Now he was playing alongside him.

Lewis said of his new friend: "As well as always cracking jokes, Ben always had time for everyone – no matter who you were or whether you had just joined or were a player who had been there for many years. He always made time for you, which I consider a very special quality to have."

The King Loses His Crown

Working at Rolls-Royce had always meant an early start for Ben, but he was not always alone when walking to work. Neil Whalen sometimes caught up with him so they could share some banter, with Rovers and City the usual topics. Neil worked at nearby Airbus so once they reached Gate Seven at Rolls-Royce, which Ben would enter, Neil's usual farewell was to plant a kiss on Ben's cheek – but not before calling him a scruff who needed a shave! For the two of them, it was a pleasant way of starting the day.

Gate Seven at Rolls-Royce held a nice memory for me. Many years ago, when most had gone home, I would go through this gate in the car with Rachel so she could use the huge car park for her driving lessons in the evening. Nowadays if I drove past at coffee break time there was a good chance Ben would be around, usually on his phone. A beep of my horn was always enough for him to look up, smile and wave before his head went back down to his phone as he attended to more important matters.

Ben was enjoying an evening out with Luke Bartley when he happened to mention in passing that he was in the process of buying a property and at some time would be looking for someone to share it with him and pay some rent. This was music to Ben's ears and he made it clear he would be well up for moving in and sharing. He became quite excited about it Luke agreed and so by the end of March it was all done and dusted.

Their new home was spacious and nicely decorated with large, well-equipped bedrooms for both of them. The first priority was a huge flat screen TV positioned at high level in the lounge, which would enable them and others to keep up to date with all the live sporting events. Our hotel at home was now closed but it seemed like another was opening up just down the road.

With one game remaining, Gifford were already champions and guaranteed a return to Premier Division One, so the last game became a special one which saw manager Martin Black make a one-off return to action. All the lads made it their goal to try and make sure he scored, so it was fitting near the end of the game when Ben seized on the chance to set up his ex-strike partner. Martin proved he had not lost his eye for goal by sticking it away to win the game, so when the final whistle sounded, the celebrations started. It had been a good few years since the last, so now was a time to enjoy. The team now had the luxury of looking forward to the next season with far more optimism.

At home, the guys were getting on even better than they could have anticipated. The household chores were shared equally and although Ben was a non-starter on the DIY front, his cooking skills earned him the title of head chef so he normally prepared and cooked the meals.

A little while later though there was a major shock in store for Barts – the very first of its kind – as the king of banter finally lost his crown. It happened after a Barts wind-up. Just before he left to go to work one morning, he hid a treasured possession that Ben cherished – his chocolate mini-eggs!! Later that day he received a call from the king himself who was in a tantrum, demanding to know where they were. An astonished Barts said: "I've seen him receive horrendous tackles week in, week out on the football pitch without losing his cool, yet there he was going mad over a pack of mini-eggs."

Later that day the chef was preparing a nice curry for their main meal – no doubt one portion would be spiked with extra hot chillies. Ouch!

For us back home, it definitely seemed very strange. Since day one back at Toronto Road, Gloria and I had never lived alone so it became a new way of life we had to adjust to. Should I reapply for our hotel licence? Perhaps not…

Work at Mitie included travelling around and sometimes out of the country, which Ben enjoyed, although sometimes it did become tiring. So along with a mate, they booked an end-of-season holiday to the

Greek island of Crete. We were especially excited about this since it's long been our favourite holiday destination, although to us it's mainly a one-place wonder – a beautiful little fishing village called Elounda.

The new hotel was booming, open all hours with no last orders being called. Weekends usually saw a full house from beginning to end, with a break on Saturday afternoons to play football. Thanks to these guys even the local bookmakers were becoming busier and wealthier than ever, especially when a major game or sporting event was taking place. The house became a gamblers' paradise, although a win was usually an unexpected bonus.

A niggling ankle injury and a couple of other minor ones sustained through wear and tear were now surfacing which affected Ben's game, but only to a certain extent. His experience and natural ability meant he soon gained a knack of being in the right place at the right time. Amongst other names – not to be mentioned – Ben was picking up the tag of poacher or fox in the box, sometimes scoring with a tap-in or a touch of fortune off his shins. Nevertheless, it was often the difference between winning or losing a game. He ended the season as top scorer yet again while Gifford not only got to the final of the cup, they won it. So after finishing fifth in the league it proved to be just what had been hoped – a great season back in the top division.

The holiday in Crete arrived at just the right time for Ben and his mate. Their luxury hotel was on the other side of the island from Elounda, although this did not stop them taking a coach excursion there one day. Included in the trip was a visit to the island of Spinalonga, which had previously been used by the Greeks as a leper colony.

A short boat trip from Elounda takes passengers over to explore the island before returning to the quaint little fishing village. This allowed the lads the chance to check out a couple of our own favourite bars and restaurants, which they did. Ben was amazed at the warm welcome he received and how our local Greek friends could instantly recognise the familiar style of speech and personality within a minute of his introduction.

First, he went into our favourite bar Babel, where he was met by Nectarius. Having introduced himself, he said: "I believe you know my parents?". The reply was instinctive. "Aaah, Clive and Gloria!" A comical conversation followed, which included free drinks. Later, he went to our favourite restaurant Anemomylos, where he was greeted by Spiros. Once again he introduced himself and said: "I believe you know my parents?" Once again the reply was instant. "Heh! Bristol Rovers!" (I wonder how he came to associate us with them). Another humorous conversation followed so both meetings provided laughs – most of them at our expense (our ears were burning). Once again the welcomes were warm and friendly as always, with Ben enjoying his short visit.

When it was time to leave, with a smile on his face, Ben promised Spiros that on his next visit he would teach him the words to *Goodnight Irene*. No doubt Spiros hoped that would be later rather than sooner.

Chapter Eleven

THIRD TIME LUCKY

With the new season well under way and Christmas approaching, Ben chose to cease house renting with Luke – mainly for financial reasons. He wanted to try and build up the funds in his savings account to help the quest for his own home. Barts completely understood this and by now the two had become even closer as mates – shortly after they met up for pre-Christmas celebrations at the Beaufort with the rest of the Gifford boys.

Ben was just entering the pub that evening when he bumped into Zoe Matthews, who was on her way out of the place as she was off for a night out with the girls. A brief greeting followed which ended with them both wishing each other a good evening before carrying on with their plans. True to form, the Beaufort provided a late, great evening of fun for the lads and with the festive period just around the corner, most of them were already becoming merry.

That year we had our first ever Christmas Day away from home. Mike and Rachel – who was now three months pregnant – provided a fun day at their own home as well as an excellent lunch, which both sets of families really enjoyed.

When we finally returned to our own home later in the evening, my head could not wait to hit the pillow. But Ben had other ideas. He sent a message to Zoe asking how she and her daughter's Christmas Day had gone. He also mentioned the possibility of meeting up one day socially for a drink. But by then Zoe had fallen asleep. She had been staying at her aunt Angela's and drinking wine to celebrate. She picked up the message on Boxing Day morning but by then felt too embarrassed to reply.

When New Year's Eve came around, family and friends arrived at our home looking to celebrate. After initial greetings, Ben was off to the Beaufort to celebrate with the villagers. By sheer coincidence, just as he arrived Zoe, along with her daughter, was leaving. Their paths had crossed yet again and once again the greeting was brief.

Zoe explains: "I worked New Year's Eve until 5pm. I picked Aaliyah up from the babysitter before meeting my friend in the Beaufort for a quick drink. Then, as I was leaving to take Aaliyah back home, I bumped into Ben, who was just arriving. We said hello but this time I just scurried away hastily. I was still embarrassed having not returned his previous text message."

The atmosphere in the Beaufort that night was one of love and friendship. Together, the villagers embraced the evening. When Big Ben chimed, everyone hugged and exchanged best wishes for the year ahead, all with smiling faces. Ben sent another message to Zoe wishing her a happy New Year. This time she replied, wishing him the same. In fact, the messaging carried on non-stop for several hours. The ice had now been broken.

On January 2, 2014 Zoe took Ben up on his offer of meeting up for a drink. This was to be their first date and Ben had it pre-planned. A 7.30pm meeting outside the new Co-op building (formerly The Parkway) before a taxi took them on their way. The destination was

Gloucester Road and of all the places it had to offer, the taxi pulled up outside The Cider Press, where they spent much of the evening.

Zoe joked: "I am far too easily impressed for that to be a suitable place for a first date, yet it was perfect from the start." Many hours were spent with conversation flowing freely and plenty of laughs. "There were no awkward silences at any point of the evening," Zoe recalled. "In fact, I realised just how easygoing and funny Ben was."

Later, it was taxi time again, this time back to the village and the home of good friend Kieron. There were other friends present too, so this gave Zoe the chance to introduce Ben to all of them. More drinks followed, along with plenty of chat, until the pair decided it was time to leave and head back home. But this time they were walking and the fresh air hit Zoe like a rock. Ben ended up having to virtually carry her home before tucking her up on the sofa and leaving quietly.

Next morning, as soon as Zoe woke up, a sense of embarrassment hit her. She genuinely thought that would be it. She certainly regretted her high alcohol consumption and worried she had made a complete fool of herself.

After a couple of hours spent moving around like a bear with a sore head, her face lightened up and she breathed a huge sigh of relief. "I picked up my phone and noticed I had a message. It was Ben. He sent such a sweet text saying that he had a really good evening and wanted to see me again."

So all was not lost. In fact, far from it. The pair later arranged to meet up that evening. Zoe thought it would be a good idea for Ben to come over after she had got Aaliyah to bed. When he did show up, he had some company and a nice surprise for Zoe. Out came a bottle of wine for her, some cans of Foster's for him and a Chinese takeaway for them to share. A chilled evening was definitely in the making. Later, amidst the fun and laughter, a more serious side came to the fore when they played a game they both loved – Monopoly. It became very competitive between the two of them – a love-hate game which neither wanted to lose, yet the enjoyment it provided meant it became a habit they could not resist.

The following day Zoe wanted to introduce Ben to Aaliyah, so in the morning he popped back around to meet her. They decided to go to McDonald's in Filton. Aaliyah found Ben very lively and humorous. The two pretty much clicked instantly and she loved the extra attention she was receiving.

At McDonald's the fun continued, especially after Aaliyah insisted she wanted an ice cream. Before walking over to stand in the queue and order, Ben dipped his nose in a pot of ketchup. Aaliyah thought it was hilarious, even more so when Ben shouted across the room asking what it was she found so funny. By now everyone in McDonald's was joining in with her laughter.

The next stop was the local park with the two of them sharing many of the rides, which Aaliyah loved. When they returned home later, it was time for her to bring out many of her games, which suddenly became far more exciting. In the evening, after her departure to bed, the Monopoly board was out again. This would decide who ended up as king or queen of the evening.

After the holiday period, the three of them went back to work and school. And although time was limited, it did not stop their friendship from blossoming. After work, Ben went back to their home to cook an evening meal and share time together, including a game or two before bedtime.

When January 6 came along and Aaliyah celebrated her sixth birthday, Zoe had already arranged a party and disco at the Bradley Stoke Hall, but also had the time-consuming job of preparing all the food. Help, though, was close at hand – and for Zoe it was heaven-sent.

"Ben not only helped, he made 80 per cent of the food," she said. "This was the day I realised just how caring he was. He really enjoyed cooking and I was thankful for all his help."

Ben did not attend but the party went well, with Aaliyah enjoying every minute. Zoe was planning to introduce Ben to all of her family on a more individual basis, but this did not stop Aaliyah from spreading word of her new friend. Most had become well aware of his name, if not his face.

Back at our home, Ben's visits were usually based on picking up more clothes from his wardrobe, which was slowly becoming bare. We were kept informed to a certain extent and told that he was living locally at a little flat in Stoke Gifford with a friend and her daughter. He assured us, with a cheeky grin, that we would meet her in the near future.

During the weeks that followed the three were virtually inseparable, which gave them the chance to learn even more about each other and help to build a loving and trusting relationship. The bonding process was now well under way. Ben and Aaliyah's relationship went from strength to strength. Zoe said: "It's fair to say he paid her a lot more attention than he did me. This became a regular thing." The same could almost be said about Aaliyah, although at the end of the day it was mummy's love and attention that would finally get her to sleep.

Our introduction was now getting closer. Every time we saw Ben we found out a little bit more. We became aware their names were Zoe and her daughter Aaliyah. I was assured she was someone I would really like. Maybe it was directed more at his mum than me, but he repeated how Zoe was different to others. "Not the norm," he said, in a kind of nervous way.

I felt that he was being protective towards her, maybe preparing us for the unexpected. But this was definitely aimed at his mum, knowing how she likes to paint a picture, trying to imagine the person she is about to meet. Nevertheless, I was now intrigued. A date was set for Friday, and as it was to be in the evening, it was to be adults only to begin with.

Gloria was hyped up when Friday arrived, so when the doorbell rang she asked me to answer it. I couldn't wait. My curiosity was about to be answered too. I couldn't wait to meet this young lady from outer space.

A New Home For All

After greetings all round and a few nervous smiles, I nipped out to the kitchen to play barman. On my return, it was good to see all three of them sitting down and already starting to chill. That was evident as I couldn't get a word in edgeways. This did give me the chance to study this young lady in an attempt to see what was different about her. The poor girl must have thought I was giving her the once over, but in truth I found her quite normal. OK, she had loads of rips in her jeans, which looked as though they had been stolen from a scarecrow, but nothing else. Ben eventually brought me into the conversation, so as the evening progressed it produced a really nice atmosphere which found all of us laid back and relaxed.

We decided a Chinese meal would be nice so I rang up and ordered a delivery. Quite a number of times, Ben secretly nodded to me with a big grin on his face. His nod then turned in the direction of Gloria and Zoe, who were by now talking for England. As gentlemen, we let them carry on without interruption. This gave us the chance to talk about more important things – football, of course. I did notice that when Ben and Zoe spoke to each other, it produced a wicked smile plus a hint of admiration in both of their glances.

The evening seemed to fly by and at the end we all promised to do it again real soon. In fact, they agreed to pop back on Sunday morning, this time with Aaliyah. So after a kiss, a smile and a wave they were off.

Gloria and I were excited over the weekend and when the three of them returned on Sunday morning, it proved we were right to be. What a lovely surprise when we met Aaliyah – a lovely little girl who spoke with such a cute voice. It was easy to see how she had become Ben's little angel. For quite a while she would not move from his side until her confidence grew enough to take part in a couple of games Ben and I played, yet from that morning on her visits became regular and she always had a broad smile on her face when she arrived. The fun and games between us grew, as did the treats for the winner – which she loved. Our home soon became a place she was excited to visit and we even inherited new names. I became "Cliver the Diver" and Gloria was "Gorgeous Glor." Our new names stuck as well.

Unknown to us, Ben really did have a romantic side. Proof came about when he arranged a Valentine's Day surprise for Zoe on February 14. The location was the Bristol Hotel in town where they both arrived with overnight bags. Zoe was the first to go into their room and discovered it lit by tealight candles with rose petals covering the bed, many gifts with her name on and two glasses of wine waiting to be drunk. A toast soon followed. Shortly afterwards they were back out again, just over the road to a place they loved. A table had been booked at the Spanish restaurant El Puerto, where they both enjoyed the atmosphere and the amazing tapas. They enjoyed it so much they vowed to return again. The weekend was completed on Sunday when all three of them came around to visit us. Our own bonding process was continuing in such a nice way and they would make regular visits midweek and on Sundays.

Zoe's sister Aimee and husband Dean soon formed a close relationship with Ben, which saw the four of them socialising together whenever time permitted. When we got to meet them it soon became very clear the two sisters had a very close and trusting relationship which they had shared throughout their lives. They both spoke very much on the same wavelength. Dean and Ben soon formed a close and comical relationship as well. They enjoyed each other's company and shared a sense of humour. What was unusual was that he never picked up a nickname.

While visiting one day in March, Ben and Zoe announced they were planning to rent their own home and they wanted my help to find a suitable place. I was more than happy to oblige. I smiled remembering that not so long ago it had taken me three attempts and I didn't want the same thing to happen to them. Stoke Gifford had to be a priority because of the location of work and Aaliyah's school, so after checking out availability with some of the local estate agents, it was interesting when a friend mentioned a local property that was about to become available. We all agreed to go and view it.

Surprisingly, with only six games remaining relegation looked likely for Gifford. Hiscox had missed a lot of games through injury – until a ray of hope came shining through. Dennis not only got to play again but found his shooting boots once more. The top scorer netted eight goals in five games, which brought the question of survival down to the final game of the season. Although he missed it because of injury, a nervous 2-2 draw saw them cling on by the skin of their teeth to remain in the top flight.

A Birthday Surprise!

The semi-detached property we were viewing had been built fairly recently and looked modern, as did the surrounding homes. It was in a cul-de-sac and had a garage to the side. Everyone appeared a little cautious as they waited for my thoughts. I was very impressed with the state of the property and its location. I even suggested that if it was good inside, then it had to be a no brainer. The mood in the camp then became positive as well as excited. The fact we could view it internally in a couple of days meant our search could be resolved in double quick time.

We were not disappointed by our look at the inside of the place – in fact, far from it. The layout ticked all the boxes. This was a house waiting to be made into a home and our feelings were unanimous. Things were even sweeter when we were given a moving in date with only two weeks to wait. Preparations were now ongoing.

In the days leading up to the move everyone was excited, none more so than one very special person who was about to see a new life begin. For Aaliyah, this move was life changing. She could now look forward to playing safely outside, hopefully with new friends. She would have a new home with much more room, but above all total love and security from two adoring parents on a regular day-to-day basis – something she had not had before but would soon get to relish.

Our van was pretty much full on the Saturday morning and although it took a couple of trips, we were fortunate the move was local, which certainly helped. Soon we were hanging shelves, reassembling beds, fixing the curtain rails and doing all the usual jobs that come with moving home. Gloria provided lots of new household goods and utensils, which would be very useful. Many of Zoe's family also called in to lend a helping hand. Her mum Fiona was soon followed by dad Paul. Of course, Aimee and Dean were present – as was a character Ben had already picked on with much humour. Aunty Angela was even looking to have his babies!

It was pretty much a full house with everyone striving to ensure the three of them would settle in nicely. Ben's luck was in. He had placed a bet on the football earlier in the day which came up trumps. That evening he showed his appreciation by treating everyone who had helped to supper at the local Pizza Hut. A long day eventually ended when we all raised a glass with a toast to wish the three of them happiness in their new home.

Monday morning saw the start of a routine which would see Ben set off to work very early while Zoe dropped Aaliyah at school before going to her own job. Ben would then finish in the nick of time to pick Aaliyah up from school before returning home. As master chef, Ben prepared the evening meals and packed lunches for the following day, although he had to be very selective when doing this. As a typical health-conscious young lady, Zoe was often on diets. "Ben would often leave me notes in my lunchbox telling me he liked me exactly as I was and to try and eat more," she said. It was further evidence of how their relationship was blossoming.

Many weeks later, Zoe decided she wanted a dog. Although Ben was not very keen, the inevitable became reality and they purchased a newborn Shih Tzu pup, which they called Albert. So along with Thomas the cat, their family was complete for the immediate future.

The new addition proved to be a lively and popular member of the family and surprisingly, it was Ben who formed the closest relationship with Albert, not only with regular feeds and cuddles but also cleaning up after the little mishaps which happened often in the early days. Even visits to our home included the little dog, who gained lots of attention with his playful ways and the tricks Ben had taught him. In fact, Albert became a main player in the surprise birthday party that Zoe had planned for Ben. Acting to her orders, it was his continual barking that persuaded Ben to take him out for a walk. So along with good friend

Rutts, who had just made a visit, the three departed for a stroll – which included the obvious trip to the Beaufort.

While they were gone it enabled family and friends to arrive and prepare for a surprise barbecue party at their home. The weather could not have been kinder. It was Saturday, June 21 – Ben had become 30 the day before. The sun was shining, the sky was blue – perfect conditions for a barbecue.

On their return from the pub, Ben was greeted with loud cheers from all. Although he looked shocked and surprised, he was soon mingling with all the guests and thanked them all for their presence. The party then got started with music playing in the background and everyone socialising and enjoying each other's company, just like one big, happy family.

I played the role of head chef at the barbecue, which became thirsty work, while Rachel – nearing the end of her pregnancy – was faced with the challenge of staying cool, calm and relaxed. Everyone joined me when I raised a toast to Ben and we filled our glasses again when I proposed another toast to honour Garth's 29th birthday, which happened to be on that day. The pair stood together acknowledging all the smiles and best wishes from all around, offering huge grins in return.

I assumed Zoe was being sponsored by Marks & Spencer since she was finding it hard to select a suitable outfit. She kept disappearing and would then return wearing a completely different one. The store would have been delighted with her fashion parade.

In truth, she had been well rewarded for all her organisational efforts, which was clearly underlined by Ben's appreciation. His arm seemed to be permanently glued around her shoulder. This was, without doubt, one of the best birthday celebrations he had experienced – with a partner he truly loved. His feelings for her were plain to see. It was very late by the time everyone departed so the big tidy up was put on hold. It was time to rest and reflect on what had been a wonderful day.

Excitement hit a high for the whole family five days later when Rachel gave birth to a baby boy and Sebastian entered our world. Ben was elated at becoming an uncle again. So shortly after mum, dad and baby returned home, the five of us visited the new arrival and his proud parents. Ben, Zoe and Aaliyah held Sebastian for the first time with a tender cuddle. Although initially unperturbed by it all, the newborn responded with some movement and facial expressions which had his admirers smiling. Before leaving, we gave our assurances we would soon return.

Bedtime duties at the new home had now been reversed, mainly due to the appearance of two new characters. Aaliyah insisted Ben should take her to bed in order to see Sooty and Sweep, who then carried out a show for her which produced fits of giggles. This carried on for quite a while until the little bear and dog became tired and wanted to go to sleep — but not before they asked to be tucked up alongside the little lady in bed. Once again two familiar words were exchanged which heralded the start of a good night's sleep: "Niber niber!"

Later in the summer, Ben updated his CV. He was looking at possible interviews with a view to furthering his career. I questioned his motives as I knew he enjoyed working at Rolls-Royce — plus the hours and location fitted in well with their current circumstances.

He was looking further ahead though and said: "Dad, the vision and plans we have for the future can't happen with the current salary I'm earning. His answer prompted me to wish him the best of luck in his search. Things were moving swiftly for the family man.

At school, Aaliyah was progressing well. She often brought work home, which saw Ben in his element. Not only did he get involved in her reading, he also set up many mathematical sums before helping and encouraging her to get the right answers. It was fun for them both, especially Aaliyah, who learned to use her fingers to help get the sums right.

Ben was cautious but excited having had an interview for a new job with a company based in Avonmouth called Safetyliftingear. Boss Mike Hughes and partner Samantha Wickens were looking to add to their successful team. They wanted a new member with the application and desire to learn about the various products on offer and to be customer orientated to deal with any queries. In return, the job could offer promotion and the salary Ben required.

Fortunately, he was offered the job. But first, out of loyalty and respect, he wanted to speak with his boss Colin, having worked with him at the first team in Rolls-Royce for over five years. The reaction he received was positive so the change was about to happen.

This was a chance to venture into pastures new, a chance that could help the family carry out their future plans together.

Having made many friends among his work colleagues at Mitie and being popular with them all, it was quite a sad farewell. In fact, the workplace became less welcoming, according to one colleague Nigel Walker.

"Ben was brilliant to be around," he said. "He was the one that brought things together, the one that made a drab day sparkle. There was never a dull moment. Nobody, but nobody, had a bad word to say about him – something that is very rare indeed. When he leaves to start his new job a void will be created which I doubt will ever be filled. He is unique."

Only time would tell if one company's loss would be another one's gain.

Chapter Twelve

THE FUTURE IS LOOKING GOOD

Shortly after the new season had started, I spoke with Ben about the latest on the football front and whether he was still enjoying it as much as ever. He believed the current group of guys were the best Gifford team he had been part of. He even thought they could have a real pop at winning the league that season. Having won the cup a couple of years before, this was his next target.

He became serious as he said this might have to be his last season for a while due to work and family commitments. With that typical grin on his face, he said he wanted to emulate his good friend John Black. Apparently the last time Gifford had won the league outright was back in 1989 when John was playing.

At work, it became very time consuming studying the catalogues to learn all about the products on offer, so to speed the process up Ben often took the books home to study in the evenings. The location of his new workplace swayed the pair to start taking driving lessons, although it was agreed that it made sense for Zoe to start first as his new job was taking its toll on his available time. They managed to purchase a nice little Citroen Saxo in preparation for the lessons.

Zoe's sister Aimee was a big help as she worked in Avonmouth as well, so Ben got into the habit of cycling to her home in the morning to grab a lift before returning home by bus later.

To help with funds and provide additional experience, I became a second driving instructor for Zoe – so when we hit the road, I insisted we had crash helmets on! Luckily, we didn't need them so my nerves remained intact. In fact, Zoe had a positive air of determination about her, yet always listened carefully and gave her best when carrying out my instructions.

Aaliyah had long been popular with many friends of similar age who lived in the close, so her first request when she got home from school was to be allowed out to play with them. This was usually granted, although once the clocks went back for the winter, the darker evenings meant her time outside became limited. She was quite upset about this, so over the next two weekends Ben set about putting some ideas into practice.

The first job was to clear out the garage and make some space before visiting family and friends to pick up some unwanted items which would be of use. The next was to carpet the cleared-out area which then had a comfy settee put in place and a corner TV unit installed with a working DVD player and television. Many games, writing pads and colouring-in books were placed on the carpet, while a large blackboard was placed on one side with some chalk for her to do some artistic designs.

A new playroom was being created so to complete it, a large board was placed at the entrance with the words "Aaliyah's amazing playhouse". Now all of her friends could come and play safely for hours – or at least until their parents came to collect them. The usual smile was back on Aaliyah's face.

Gifford were doing exceptionally well sitting at the top of the league, although their next game saw them face local rivals and current league champions Little Stoke.

Typical banter was exchanged just before kick-off when Little Stoke captain Ashley Coles, with a grin on his face, warned Hiscox: "Watch out mate – when I do get to tackle you I might break your legs!" Hiscox returned the smile and retorted: "You'll have to catch me first, Colesy!"

As expected, it was a close and fierce encounter until Dennis tapped in the first goal. It got even better for him late in the game when the ball rebounded off his shin before finding the back of the net to seal a 2-0 victory. Neither may have been contenders for goal of the season, but that did not bother his jubilant team-mates. With big smiles they hugged each other and celebrated three more vital points in their quest to become champions.

The driving lessons paid off when Zoe passed her test on December 2. The fact they were now mobile was welcomed by them both, as it made a big difference to their lifestyle. As a family they could now travel independently to visit friends and family. For Zoe, the icing on the cake was that she could now pick Ben up from work and he could prepare and cook dinner again.

But evenings in the household were becoming quite hectic, especially during school time. Aaliyah had to stick to a strict sleep routine for health reasons and she much preferred to use the bath rather than the shower. This meant washing and drying her long hair became very time consuming. In an effort to save time, Ben managed to encourage her to use the shower – but only after slipping into his trunks and joining her, which produced the extra bit of confidence required.

Just as her mum did when she was younger, Aaliyah suffers from epilepsy, which can cause seizures and at its extreme cause her to lose control of her limbs and shake. Ben had been made aware of this having witnessed it happen, so he knew what action to take should it happen. Daily medication was helping to control the condition, although medical staff still had to find the correct levels she needed.

While in school one day, Aaliyah was suddenly taken ill and consequently taken to Frenchay Hospital, where she remained overnight for observation. Thankfully, her mum was allowed to take her back home the next day. Ben was given permission to leave work early to go home and see her so his mum provided an urgent pick up. On his way home, he insisted on calling into Poundland and managed to muster £10 worth of change, allowing him to buy 10 items for her.

After receiving a big embrace, she was excited to receive her 10 gifts. But that was just a front because her real happiness was over the fact she was back home with the two people who adored her the most.

Joe's Got A New Fan!

Excitement was at an all-time high when Christmas arrived. It was Ben's favourite time of the year and a new tradition was about to be introduced to the two ladies. After Aaliyah's departure to bed the gifts, which were usually placed under the tree, were arranged differently. Santa had other ideas so he decided to put presents for the two adults on the lounge chairs, keeping the settee free for Aaliyah's gifts. The room was ready and all was silent – although that wouldn't last for long when the little lady became the first to enter.

Up until that point, Ben and Rachel had always spent Christmas Day with us and that year was to be no exception. Without doubt it was certainly our happiest and proudest as for the first time it included both of their little families. It was a house full of love and appreciation. Aaliyah was still full of excitement about the presents she had received earlier while Sebastian, with his little thumb in his mouth to aid concentration, just watched and took it all in his stride.

My efforts at cooking lunch were rewarded with compliments from all and it was interesting, sitting around the lunch table, when Ben finally managed to get everyone to agree to a verbal contract. For quite a while we had tried to arrange a family holiday together, but with work commitments and other issues we had never got around to doing it. Ben's determination worked when we all agreed to keep the last week in March free.

Now it was down to the main organiser in our household to finalise the booking arrangements and since this was to be our first complete family holiday away together with our two youngest members, this was to be our treat. After checking out numerous options, Gloria booked a huge cottage in Weymouth. We later paid a visit to take a look and we weren't disappointed. In fact, following our revelations, we were all very excited.

For Ben and the girls, New Year's Eve was spent at Aimee and Dean's home, where an evening of fun saw everybody wearing a mask to hide their identities. The two sisters then provided a Beyoncé dance-off competition while Ben took on the role of judge. He was so impressed he ended up joining in with the pair before announcing his verdict – a draw! A smiling Dean agreed with the decision and shortly afterwards, all four raised a glass to health and happiness for the year ahead.

Plans for Aaliyah's seventh birthday had been ongoing so when she woke up on the morning of January 10 she was excited to see her gifts and cards. The last card she opened was from her two biggest admirers, although she struggled to read it in full so Ben took over and read it to her. He revealed they were all off to London for the weekend to stay overnight in a hotel. Zoe's cousin Richard, who lived in London, was waiting to meet them and would act as tour guide to show them many of the attractions.

Ben then produced three theatre tickets for a performance of *Charlie and the Chocolate Factory*, which was a big favourite of hers. The birthday surprise was greeted with huge smiles and hugs, but there was not much time to spare. The car had already been packed and was waiting to go. The journey would allow time to reveal the places they were looking to visit. The atmosphere was full of excitement and anticipation.

The weekend certainly lived up to expectations. The sights and the stores were fascinating, while the show offered many laughs and proved to be amazing. They returned home late the following day, tired but happy.

The following Saturday, Stoke Gifford's match was called off at the last minute, which was a shame because a surprise visitor had returned to his old stomping ground to watch the team play. Another reason for the visit was to see an old mate and on that front he was not disappointed. Lorenzo greeted Ben with a hug. It had been a while but they were both chuffed to see each other again. There was lots to talk about so it was off to the Beaufort for a chat and a catch-up. Their situations had changed so much it made for fascinating conversation, especially when Lorenzo announced he was now married with a daughter. Ben was overjoyed to hear this and then revealed that he too was in a similar situation – it just wasn't official. This created laughter between the two of them.

When Lorenzo had to leave, they shook hands and said they would have to meet up again in the near future. Shortly afterwards, just as Ben was about to depart, another good friend turned up in the shape of Gemma, so another catch-up was on the way. Their chat was good humoured but turned slightly more serious when Ben confided to her about his current situation and just how good things in his life were. He even joked that he had finally grown up, which brought a smile to

Gemma's face. She was pleased to see him so happy and felt it was well deserved. When they eventually parted, it was with smiles and hugs all round.

The Bristol Hotel was their Valentine's venue once again on February 14. True to their word, the couple went back to the El Puerto restaurant and sat and discussed how their year had unfolded, which lit up both their faces. Excitement then grew as plans for the year ahead were discussed, the main one being a new addition to the family. A baby Hiscox was top of their wish list and they agreed to start trying in the very near future. They even hoped that by the time they were back in the restaurant next year, their wishes would have been granted. The mutual love and respect they showed each other was a sign of their total commitment.

In total confidence, Ben was told some worrying news after meeting up with his good friend Westy, who was worried about the health of his younger sister Georgina. Ben was good friends with George, so he was shocked and saddened by the disclosure. He assured Jamie that the much-loved young lady was strong and told him not to lose faith. The two were keeping their fingers firmly crossed for her speedy recovery.

For many years, I had accompanied Gloria when she went to see Joe Longthorne perform live. She had booked tickets to see him at Weston-super-Mare's Playhouse Theatre on March 11. During that day at work, I encountered various problems with the installation I was working on and it became obvious I would need to work on into the evening in order to stick to the schedule as other tradesmen were due in the next day. Sure enough, I was in the doghouse when I had to ring Gloria to explain. It was somewhat ironic that Rachel, a perfect substitute, had her own commitments to Sebastian so couldn't go. My feeling of guilt was compounded when Gloria rang back later to say she now wouldn't be going.

To my complete surprise, I received a call from Ben later in the evening. He was ringing from Weston. "You owe me one for this, dad," he said jokingly. I replied: "Mate, you have saved my bacon!" Gloria had called him on the off chance and he had agreed to join her. It was the first time he had even seen Joe Longthorne. A few days later we met up and Ben said how much he had enjoyed the show. He even said he was thinking about joining Joe's fan club. I was astounded... but then I saw the cheeky grin. Enough said!

Ben was progressing really well at work, along with his office buddies Megan, Kara, Lucy and Luke. He was gaining a reputation for being the first one to answer the phone, which the others found humorous. The icing on the cake came just before our cottage holiday when Mike and Samantha invited him into their office to express their delight with his efforts to date. They agreed that on his return from holiday they would discuss a rise in salary, which they both felt was deserved. Mike explained: "You could really see that Ben got a buzz from selling and solving customers' problems and that takes will and determination. Having had no knowledge of our products, within a short time he was outselling every other member of our sales team. Amazing!"

The plans that had been set out a while before were falling firmly into place and the future was looking good, which justified all the effort that had been made. Ben had already saved a substantial amount of money towards an engagement ring and was certainly looking to propose in the near future, although for now he was happy to wait for the right time.

Next up on the agenda was the family holiday – a nice chance to relax and recharge the batteries before returning to carry on the good work.

On The Road To Recovery

Gloria and I checked in to Laurel Cottage on Friday, March 20, 2015. We were thrilled with all the facilities it had to offer – large bedrooms with en suite and bathroom plus a huge dining area, kitchen and lounge. I was in my element in the amazing kitchen, while Gloria was in her element tuning in our digital radio to find Radio Bristol, which was broadcasting the evening kick-off between Bristol Rovers and Aldershot.

After work, Ben and the girls joined us just in time for us to eat together in the dining room while listening to the game, which the Gas won 3-1. When the final whistle blew, we all stood up and raised a glass before singing *Goodnight Irene*. What a nice way to start our holiday.

Rachel, Mike and Sebastian joined us on Saturday. Everyone was excited about the lovely cottage, as well as being in each other's company. The dining room, in particular, with its long table and chairs, became a popular place for everyone to chill out and relax, usually accompanied by a full glass. The days provided quality time for everyone, with beach time at Ringstead, Lulworth Cove and Weymouth – plus dropping our lines around the harbour area, which Aaliyah especially enjoyed.

The fun fair on the Esplanade soon became a favourite. The dodgems provided a challenge which saw Ben and Aaliyah take on Mike and me. We lost by five hits to four so the ice creams were on us as the losers.

Early mornings were very enjoyable. Ben came down quietly with Aaliyah, which allowed Zoe a lie-in. Likewise, I looked after Sebastian to allow Mike and Rachel the rare luxury of a lie-in. True to form, Gloria had a lie-in naturally. Bless!

After breakfast we'd go outside to the back of the cottage for a game of bowls on the lovely grass lawn. The games were taken very seriously – but somehow Aaliyah always seemed to win. One evening, Ben produced a quiz. The prize for the winner was 10 free ride vouchers at the fun fair. Twenty questions were based on the film *Frozen*. As hard as we all tried, the outright winner – with 20 out of 20 correct – was again Aaliyah.

Monday evening was the last we would all be together so Gloria booked a table for a farewell meal at The Springhead pub near the cottage. We wanted to cover the cost with the least amount of fuss, so just before leaving I called out to everyone asking if they could join us in the hallway. With Sebastian and Aaliyah in the middle, we had a big group hug while I explained my intention. The love and appreciation shown by all made it a moment to treasure.

After an enjoyable time at the pub, we returned to the cottage. Once the young ones were tucked up in bed, it was time for my quiz for adults (one that I had doctored). The atmosphere changed like the wind. It started with laughter, then took on a slightly more serious note – especially from Gloria. Her tone of voice was rising in disbelief at the amount of correct answers the others were getting. After heated exchanges with the quizmaster, she even claimed the questions had been fixed. As if!

The game was up though when I asked who played their home games at Brisbane Road and Zoe came up with the answer – Leyton Orient. That was the moment Ben cracked up. He knew she had no idea about football and cared about it even less. Knowing me, he put two and two together. We all saw the funny side of it though – even Gloria once she had calmed down.

The following morning we were all off to West Bay. Gloria was well aware that many of the local buildings had been used in the TV series

Broadchurch, so we went to check them out. Shortly after lunch it was time to bid farewell to Ben and the girls. They had to go back to work and school the next day, so we arranged to meet up over the weekend before wishing them a safe journey home.

While driving to work the following morning, Aimee was in conversation with Ben. He said how much he was looking forward to the holiday they had all booked together, along with husband Dean, at Ladram Bay in Devon later that summer. He carried on by saying how good the holiday we'd just been on was and how much he'd enjoyed it. He confided: "Aim, I had a moment. We were all on the beach at Lulworth Cove. I was just looking around at all the family together and seeing everyone so happy. It really does make you realise what life is all about." This prompted a smile from Aimee.

Later that day, after finishing work, Zoe visited her local surgery to have the contraceptive implant in her arm removed in preparation for expanding the family. The pair were both excited about this.

I was back to work myself on Saturday, March 28, happy knowing it was only for a short day. I arrived back home at 2.45pm to grab some lunch. A while later I received a call from Zoe who said she had just received a call saying Ben had been injured playing football, although she did not know to what extent. I assured her I was close at hand if I was needed, knowing I had to pop to B&Q which was only a few minutes away from where Ben was playing. I told her to ring Gloria with any further news since she was concerned.

As I approached Stoke Gifford in my van, Gloria rang me and sounded very distressed. I could barely make out a word she was saying so I turned into North Road and parked up in the Beaufort car park. She then slowly explained that Zoe had picked her up and they were both on their way to Southmead Hospital. She carried on saying Ben had sustained a head injury and was being taken there. I was less than a minute away from the ground so I decided to nip round there. But before I even moved I looked up to see three ambulances speed past me with lights flashing. It was obvious that Ben was inside one of them so I hastily made my way to the hospital, a very worried man.

Once there, I met up with Gloria, Zoe and Ross Matthews, who had been only metres away from the incident when it happened. He told us the details of what had happened, which sounded horrific.

We had to wait a couple of hours before seeing Ben and while alone and sharing our concerns, Zoe showed a text message she had received from him shortly before kick-off time. Apparently he had never texted her before a game in the past. The short message said: "I love you gorgeous! xxx" In turn, we gave her a hug and reassurance that he was in the best place to help him deal with what had happened.

We eventually got to see Ben, who was in a comatose state and connected to lots of tubes and breathing equipment. It was very frightening. He was later taken to an intensive care ward where only two visitors could be present at a time.

Rachel and Mike arrived to join us, just before we were told that X-rays had shown Ben had fractured the back of his skull in two places. He also had bruising to the front of his brain, but on a positive note the main part of his brain had not been bruised. We were advised that a full recovery was possible in the long term, although the next 48 hours were critical to his recovery. We all hugged, extremely worried and concerned, but we spoke positively. We were now all in this trauma together and would see it through together – hopefully with a silver lining at the end.

Later that evening we were introduced to a nurse, who assured us he would be at Ben's bedside throughout the night. Shortly afterwards, the others left to return home and later Ben came out of his coma but remained connected to all the equipment required to support his serious condition. Before I eventually left, I shook hands with the nurse and then went back home myself – although sleep was the last thing on my mind.

We returned the following morning at 10am and were shown to the main waiting room for the intensive care ward. From here, any two of us could visit Ben's bedside, so we took it in turns. The nursing staff had now changed and Ben was being given mental tests on the hour. This involved the nurse talking to him loudly. The aim was to try and get a response, but progress was not looking good. During the afternoon, two young nurses were monitoring him, but they disappeared after the hourly tests.

Then we gained a massive breakthrough. Zoe and I were alone with him trying to carry out our own verbal questioning. Zoe shouted out a question which made Ben respond. It was a tired, slurred response – but it was music to our ears. We hugged each other after our achievement and Zoe explained with a smile that she often shouted at Ben during the night if he was snoring loudly and it usually worked. This time the tactic certainly did work.

We continued asking him various questions, this time in a more normal tone of voice, and we were getting answers. They were slow, tired replies but we were excited about the progress we were making. At one stage I had to take steps back and turn away as Zoe and Ben exchanged some loving words. Suddenly I felt the largest lump in my throat that I had ever experienced.

Later in the afternoon, Ben was becoming restless and asking to use the loo. We were given a bed pot but Zoe's attempts to encourage him to use it failed. Shortly afterwards, he attempted to get out of bed, although I managed to restrain him – only temporarily though. As I walked away in search of a nurse to make them aware of the situation, he managed to pull off all of his tubes before jumping out of bed and literally running off down the ward.

Zoe and I raced after him pleading that he should stop. When he reached a door, he did. Then he opened it and went into a washroom containing Belfast sinks, cleaning products, mops and buckets. By the time we reached him, he was producing a huge stream into a yellow bucket. As soon as it was finished, so was all his strength. We even had to get him back to bed in a wheelchair that Zoe requested.

Between us we both changed the bedding, as well as his gown, which was soiled with blood. We then helped him out of the wheelchair and back into bed, where a nurse reconnected all his tubes. We then saw him resting again comfortably.

When Rachel and Mike came to his bedside, they sang a few quiet verses of *Goodnight Irene*, which were greeted with a smile and a few softly spoken words. Although tired, he was still able to acknowledge us and converse quietly.

At the end of the evening, I was again alone with the nurse from the previous night and before I left, we made another breakthrough. Having not eaten since he'd been in the hospital, the nurse woke Ben and insisted he must try to eat a small fruit jelly he'd just taken from the fridge. But Ben was tired and very reluctant. The nurse then spoke firmly, telling him that I was going to feed it to him. Slowly but surely he obliged and after the final spoonful, he tapped his tummy and said: "Sorted!" Another achievement had been made.

Shortly afterwards, he went back to sleep and was looking comfortable, so again I shook hands with the nurse before departing. This time, my journey back home was a far more pleasant one.

When I got there, I even managed a first – with Gloria's help. I wrote a long text message with an update of the situation and managed to send it to numerous family and friends – without having to repeat it

25 times! In the message I confessed that the jelly had given me more joy and satisfaction than any other meal I had ever prepared for Ben, which probably gave most a laugh.

Even later, we received a call from John Gibbs, who assured us he was convinced Ben was going to be alright. He firmly believed he could and would pull through, which was comforting to hear.

The call I received the next morning was even more comforting and had me beaming like a Cheshire cat when it became clear Ben really was – on the road to recovery!

Chapter Thirteen

BANKING ON THE FIFTH TEST

Between us, visiting arrangements for Monday were finalised. Zoe would be first in, followed by Gloria. I went to work in the morning, then looked after Sebastian in the afternoon, which allowed Rachel the chance to call in.

At 10.30am I received a call that not only brought a smile to my face but was like a breath of fresh air. It was Zoe, who explained that Ben had not only sat up and eaten some breakfast, but he had earlier asked the nurse where his little girl Aaliyah was. He even enquired about his mobile phone.

Hospital staff must have been impressed with his condition because he was later transferred from intensive care to a high-dependency ward, which he shared with three others and had one nurse looking after all four.

In the afternoon, along with Gloria and Rachel, many of the Gifford boys were now able to call in and see their mate. The greeting was standard, with smiles and a bit of ribbing, which lightened the situation. A few were still around to witness the customary farewell when it was time for Zoe to go.

After exchanging kisses, she felt embarrassed to say the usual two words and headed for the door. Just before she reached it, Ben kept up the tradition and shouted: "Love you!" Zoe replied "Love you too!" before leaving hastily. When it was time for the Gifford boys to depart, their farewell words were rather different. "See you tomorrow, me old mucker!"

Just before leaving, Rachel encouraged her brother to eat some fruit and drink some squash she had brought in for him, which he promised to do. Like her mum, they both noticed he was beginning to tire so hugs and kisses were exchanged before they departed.

I arrived in the evening as the last visitor of the day. Entering the ward, I noticed the other three patients were sitting up, one reading, one writing while the other one – who acknowledged me – was drinking tea or coffee. Ben was asleep, so I sat beside his bed. Shortly afterwards he woke up and realised it was me. His lifetime greeting followed, although he said it quietly and slowly. His eyes were extremely swollen, as if he hadn't slept for a week.

I helped him sit up before he said softly: "Dad, I think I'm ready to go home now." I assured him the progress he was making was amazing and he certainly would be going home soon. But as the evening progressed, he appeared to become agitated, uncomfortable and often tried to rub the back of his head, which still must have been very painful.

He wanted to use the loo, so I went out and found the nurse and asked for assistance. Together we helped him to the toilet. He walked slowly, swaying from one side to the other, finding it hard to keep his balance. After standing over the loo for a minute or so, he declared that he couldn't go. Then he walked in a drunken-like state over to the basin on his own. As we watched, he turned on the mixer tap before bending his head down to drink the water. Finally, we encouraged and helped him back into bed.

For quite a while he tossed and turned, finding it hard to get comfortable. I suggested he lay on his side with a pillow supporting the back of his head. Luckily, this seemed to provide some comfort and he went back to sleep.

He remained comfortable for the next couple of hours so I decided to leave. I walked over to the nurse and explained that his current position seemed to be the most comfortable, so she assured me that if he needed to get up, she would help him return to it.

As I wished goodnight to the nurse, Ben raised his head and looked over to me as if it was him I was saying goodnight to. He then put his head back on the pillow. Even so, I hung around for a short while in case he woke up to speak. But this didn't happen so I left quietly.

Walking out of the hospital, I could not help feeling worried. As requested, I texted Zoe and Rachel and told them both of my concerns. After all the encouraging events of the day, I expected to see Ben in a far more healthy state. I had just left him with no bedside nurse, unlike the other two nights. She might not be close at hand or even aware if he needed assistance. Is it me? Am I being over-protective?

Once I got back home, on reflection I realised it had been a long, tiring but progressive day in his recovery. I remembered how important and crucial the last 48 hours had been. We were told they were critical and he had come through with flying colours. Maybe I should be more thankful about his improvement. With the medication he was receiving, I suppose his condition had to be expected. Hopefully he should soon be on a par with the other three patients in his ward – although knowing Ben, if he was sat up relaxing then his priority would be texting on his phone. Hopefully a good night's sleep would do him a power of good and tomorrow he would look and feel a lot better for it. How I hope when Zoe calls me it brings out my Cheshire cat smile again.

On March 31, 2015 at 4.40am we had a phone call from the hospital advising us to come in straight away. Ben had suffered two seizures during the night.

After a mad rush, when we arrived we were escorted past his bed and could not see him because the side curtain was drawn. We did see many hospital staff around his bed deliberating as we were led to a waiting room in the ward, where we were met by Zoe, Aimee and Aunty Angela. We all embraced and comforted each other, although we were in a very nervous state. But as time passed I became more positive and hopeful that Ben was going to pull through.

After two hours, Zoe's patience was being stretched to the limit so she decided to leave the room and speak to the desk receptionist on the ward. She insisted we should be given an update on Ben's condition, so half an hour later a surgeon came into the room.

We were told that Ben was being taken down to theatre. The seizures had caused high pressure around the brain so they were looking to try and measure the extent of this and hopefully bring it under control. We were advised the operation would take about half an hour.

An hour or so later, there was still no news. The tension in the room was immense, but all the while I felt that no news was good news. The longer it went on, the more likely the news would be good.

Zoe's dad Paul arrived, Rachel and Mike were on their way.

Another half an hour passed before a surgeon in a blue gown came into the room. He asked what was the latest we had been told about Ben's condition. Immediately I spoke and the others remained silent. I assumed this guy was a specialist, drafted in to deal with Ben's condition, so I thought I would assist him by outlining all the facts, from the outset to the present time. I hoped this would help him diagnose or determine the best medical solutions to help Ben's recovery.

My explanation carried on for a good couple of minutes. The surgeon was listening intently without speaking, yet he appeared to be taking everything I was saying on board. I genuinely believed the information I was giving him would help him make the best diagnosis since he still did not say a word.

Suddenly, Zoe interrupted me and asked: "Is he dead?" I turned my head to her in disbelief. How could she even contemplate that? The guy would have said ages ago if that was the case.

I then turned back to the surgeon. To my complete horror, he was nodding his head.

Everyone in the room started screaming. They were hysterical. For the first time in ages, I became silent. Nothing to say. This can't be true. He's got it wrong. This is my boy. No way. It can't be. Not Ben. Never.

As the noise level started to quieten down, I felt numb, speechless. The surgeon apologised for being the bearer of such sad news. Questions were thrown at him. Why? What? When? How come?

Gloria tried to hug me but I couldn't respond. I had no strength. If I had hugged her back, it would be evidence that I had accepted my boy had died. Never!

Shortly after, Rachel and Mike arrived. They immediately carried out a group hug with Zoe and Gloria. This encouraged me to join them. It was just as we all had done eight days earlier, only this time we were all shaking and full of tears. This time our group hug was missing one main player – our son, her brother, his brother-in-law and her future husband. Everything that was going on around me seemed like a blur, a bad dream. Please just let me wake up and realise it was just a nightmare.

Later, we were taken to another part of the hospital and shown into another waiting room. Ben was taken into a ward close to the room. He still had the assistance of the ventilating equipment so his body was breathing, as if he was doing it naturally. Once again we were allowed in twos to sit at his bedside. He appeared to be sleeping peacefully. His body and skin looked completely natural. His hand felt the same as it always had. I still hoped there was a chance he might wake up. You never know with Ben.

John and Mark arrived shortly afterwards, then a lady came into the room and introduced herself. She spoke for quite a while expressing her deepest sympathy and sorrow. Suddenly though, her words hit me like a bombshell. "Would you be prepared to donate Ben's organs to help others?"

Hang on a minute. Talk about run before you can walk. I was only talking with my son last night and now you want his organs? What is going on?

The debate started and it seemed to go on and on, although I could not get my head around it. How can we even begin to consider something such as this at such an early stage? Then I felt anger, although I just sat with my head in my hands.

Shortly afterwards, a nurse opened the door to announce we had visitors. It was the Gifford boys. This inspired me. It gave me the strength I needed to get up off the chair and go and meet them.

I insisted on being alone. In turn, I hugged each and every one before taking them, to see Ben. In pairs, they went to his bedside, fighting hard to control their emotions. After all, a member of their family had just left them.

When I returned to the room, I found myself able to talk to the lady, who was a specialist in organ donation. As parents, the final decision was left to us. Of course, we both agreed for Ben's organs to be used for the sake of others. It was the right thing to do. Those would have been Ben's wishes as well, bless him.

But first, by law, the specialist neurosurgeon had to carry out five tests on Ben as proof of death and he required two of us to witness them. Gloria was too distraught so Zoe accompanied me. We sat either side of the bed so we could hold his hand while the tests were carried out.

The first four tests didn't go well, maybe as expected. My life, my hopes, my everything were resting on this last test. In my mind, I became desperate. I made a pact with God to take me and allow Ben to live.

Then came the fifth test, when the ventilator would momentarily be taken off to see if Ben could breathe on his own. I squeezed his hand to encourage him. "Come on my best mate, you can do this. Mate, come on. Please? For me?"

There was no response until the ventilator was finally reconnected.

It felt like my world had ended. Once again I became completely numb. No energy. Completely shattered.

Thankfully, Zoe helped me up off the chair before we embraced for what seemed like an eternity. We then very slowly started walking away. I took one last look around to take a look at my son. What a bloody handsome young man.

Gloria was waiting outside for me. This time, we hugged. And hugged. And hugged. Thirty-odd years ago, that young man spayed his mum when he came into our world. Now here we are saying farewell to him. How cruel.

Slowly we made our way from the hospital. The only difference this time was that we wouldn't be returning.

Later back home, at 11.30pm, I had a phone call from the organ donation specialist. She explained to me she had taklen the decision to close down the ventilator keeping Ben alive. She explained: "His little heart was under too much stress and could take no more." I thanked her for keeping us informed.

The day had come to an end. It finished just as it had started. By far the very worst in my entire life.

Chapter Fourteen

OUR BOY MADE US PROUD

The following morning we met the Gifford boys at the football ground in North Road. They were assembled together waiting as we approached the pitch. As we got closer, we could see numerous cards and bunches of flowers up against the clubhouse wall. We were told some were positioned in the very spot where Ben had hit the wall with his head.

Over the next days and weeks, hundreds of cards and bunches of flowers were placed along the clubhouse wall in a sea of bright colours. Local clubs and football supporters pinned their own coloured shirts to the wall in a mark of respect. Press coverage reported the incident in detail. The words "tragic freak accident" became a constant headline, a label that seemed to stick. The term was used consistently by national and local papers for days afterwards.

By the time word got around, it left the whole village in total shock. This was, after all, the villagers' own adopted son. The community decided to meet up that evening at the Beaufort to pay their respects. The pub was soon heaving inside, which meant some spilled out into the open air. Later, when a bell rang loudly, everyone stood and raised their glass to Ben Hiscox – a much-loved and true friend of them all. Till takings broke all records that night, such was his popularity.

Another first was soon to follow, thanks mainly to public demand and total support across the whole city which proved to be truly humbling. Bristol Rovers were due to play a home game on Good Friday, April 3 and huge numbers were united in their plea for the club to hold a tribute to Ben in his memory. This had never happened for an amateur footballer before, yet 24 hours later the club announced that they would honour the request. How fitting that the club he loved and supported were now paying him the ultimate respect.

So on April 3, Rovers took on Chester City and the Good Friday crowd contained many who had never been to a game of professional football before. So many City fans forgot their loyalty and so many others made a first visit to the stadium to support a very special young man.

Both teams came out of the tunnel and walked straight across the pitch to where we were standing. In a line, the players all bowed their heads while we as a family, along with the Gifford lads, filed out onto the pitch. Once we were all in a line, the customary warm-up and run around followed before both teams then stood around the centre circle. Club announcer Nick Day then read out a tribute to Ben, which ended with the words: "The family would hopefully like to dedicate promotion this season to Ben."

With everyone in the ground standing, a minute's applause began while we all stood in a regimented line. Suddenly, my emotions got the better of me and I broke ranks. I just had to walk across the pitch while turning full circle with my hands in the air clapping. I wanted to witness and show my appreciation to everyone in the crowd for showing their respect

Finally, I made my way over to the Blackthorn End, the terrace where my boy had spent so many happy hours. The reception I received will live with me forever. I looked up to the sky and thought: "All this is for you Ben." A little later Ben Bennett told me the decibel level trebled when I did that.

As I returned to my place, both managers greeted me with a hug. How kind. As a family, this was a truly humbling experience for all of us. The club had made us proud – and we were certainly proud to be classed as Gasheads. The tribute was complete when Rovers went on to win 5-1 to take another step towards promotion.

I later met up with then chairman Nick Higgs to express my sincere thanks for giving us as a family what was a rare opportunity. He said we deserved it and stressed that Rovers were a family club. They certainly proved it.

Back home, we now faced the dreaded task of arranging the funeral. Popularity, as well as size and tradition, swayed all of us, including Zoe, who was now part of our family, to agree that Westerleigh Crematorium would be the most suitable location, although we had to look for at least double the usually allocated time. The date of April 15 was set and I was honoured when the Gifford boys met up with me and asked if they could be pallbearers at the service.

We all felt it would be fitting to start and end the day at the Beaufort. This would not only provide an opportunity for all who wished to be present on the day, but was also our way of keeping it in the village – the village he truly loved. Our only request was that bright colours were to be worn as we wanted it to be a celebration of Ben's life.

When we arrived at the Beaufort, the limousine cars were waiting. The one carrying the coffin had blue and white flowers shaped into a long cross on the top, while to the sides were a number of other shapes and designs, including a football. At the rear was a huge Rovers shirt, again made with blue and white flowers, which produced a colourful display.

As we pulled away, I couldn't help but stare at the coffin. Inside was my boy. It felt so surreal. I will never forget the sight as we pulled into the Westerleigh grounds. Several hundred had turned up to pay their respects. It was like a sea of blue and white. The majority would not even be able to get into the church, although external loudspeakers meant they could listen to the service outside. The minister, Rev Steven Hawkins, wore a blue and white scarf around his neck and provided a truly memorable service. Tributes were read out, first from Mark, then from Dean, who was speaking on behalf of Zoe after she wrote the words. Best mate Garth wrote and read out his tribute before my new good friend Rick Johansen read out the realistic and beautiful words he had written two days after Ben's passing, called *Slate Grey Skies*. The tributes ended with one I wrote, which Steven read out impeccably. Following the blessing, we all ushered our way out to the sound of *Goodnight Irene*. There was not one dry eye in the place. The press and media were there to note the occasion, which had been given prominent coverage. The sky remained blue from early morning to dusk, which seemed almost like kind respect for the celebration of Ben's life.

Back at the Beaufort, hundreds were outside – mainly because it was full inside. It gave all a chance to mingle and reminisce about past times with Ben. It was easy to spot the ones that were – they were the ones with big smiles on their faces. For many hours I made an effort to meet and thank all those I was not really aware of. I wanted to learn about their friendship with Ben. All the time in my arms I had a companion who did want to leave my side, which was good enough for me so there was no way I was going to let him. Although a little shy, Sebastian found it fascinating meeting and greeting so many new faces. Later on in the evening, in common with many other youngsters, he also enjoyed watching a fireworks display on the green opposite the Beaufort.

When the evening came to an end, it seemed strange wandering around looking at so many empty chairs and tables. The pub was deserted and quiet, but once again another record was set at the tills.

Our plans for Ben's ashes were put on hold as we waited for permission from the church and the parish council for our wishes to be carried out. But with backing from the entire village, our fingers were firmly crossed.

Zoe and Aaliyah's lives had changed so much since meeting Ben, we were determined to help them carry on living to the standard they had been, which is exactly what Ben would have wanted.

With this in mind and with huge help from family and friends, fundraising was very much on the agenda. Leading the way on behalf of Safetyliftingear were Mike and Samantha, who gained vast donations and sponsorship from many business clients as well as staging numerous events to raise money. The culmination came at their own warehouse in Avonmouth, which staged an evening of fun and mayhem including a special appearance by the Somerset Paddies, an amazing West Country group very much in the mould of The Wurzels. Sam's dad is a member of the group and they had everyone singing and dancing along merrily. Through all their efforts, Mike and Sam helped to raise in excess of £10,000.

The bank holiday of May 4 saw the Ben Hiscox Benefit Match take place at Manor Farm. John Black fielded a team representing Manor Farm who had previously played alongside Ben. Martin Black formed the opposition with the current Stoke Gifford lads. The day included many other attractions, which were attended and enjoyed by hundreds. John Gibbs, especially, worked tirelessly helping to organise the day, which raised more than £6,000. Manor Farm's chairman Geoff Sellek kindly offered complete use of all the facilities at the ground and also confirmed that the club's top scorer at the end of the season would be presented with the Ben Hiscox Memorial Trophy something that would continue on an annual basis.

Friday, May 8 saw Stoke Gifford have their biggest game for 28 years. On the final day of the season, the lads were in with a chance of winning the league title and finishing as champions. Ironically, their opponents were Mangotsfield Sports – which happened to be the team they played on March 28. They too could be crowned champions if they won the game – although a draw would be enough for Gifford.

Before the game kicked off, one of the Gifford lads was reflecting: "We'd have won this league weeks ago if Hiscox had still been around." It was an evening game and I arrived at Mangotsfield after work to take a seat next to John Gibbs. It was half-time and Gifford were losing 1-0.

In the second half my adrenaline refused to let me stay seated so in an effort to provide vocal encouragement, I walked up and down near the touchline in an effort to keep up with play. I found myself shouting instructions to the lads, which gave me a sense of guilt – especially as manager Martin Black was over the other side of the pitch. But deep down I knew he would be fine with my vocal backing as we were now all in this together.

When Gifford's young full-back burst into the box, he was about to shoot at goal but clearly fouled. "Penalty!" I shouted at the top of my voice. The referee agreed and pointed to the spot and the kick went in. 1-1.

As the game entered stoppage time, the lads were under the utmost pressure. Unbelievably, the ref added nine minutes, although it seemed more like nine hours. Keeper Lee Ballard had been magnificent, but for how much longer?

At last the ref blew for full-time and I was on the pitch like a whippet racing over to congratulate the players and the manager. They had finished off what had been started. This is what Ben really wanted for the team – for them to be crowned champions.

Emotions kicked in as each and every player told me they had achieved this for Ben. They were determined not to let him down – and they certainly didn't. The lads insisted I join them in the changing rooms and soon afterwards in the showers the usual songs were being belted out – similar to what had started 12 years before, only now the creator was missing. I did sense his presence around though. He was enjoying this. I certainly felt the lads had a 12th man out there on the pitch, defending our goalmouth. There could be no other explanation how the ball failed to find the back of our net.

But celebrations had to be kept to a minimum because the date had long been set for the club's end-of-season party at the Hilton Hotel in Almondsbury. Ben had already ensured it was penned into our diary so we went along as a family. We were all made very welcome by the players and their partners. Throughout the evening, while music was being played, a big screen to the side of the dancefloor was showing various photos of the lads, ladies and Ben enjoying fun times together. Broad smiles were visible on everyone.

Zoe and I collected two awards on Ben's behalf – top goalscorer, of course, and the players' own award of player of the year. It was an emotional but enjoyable evening, and one which we were all grateful to be part of.

Just over a week later, on May 17, our destination was Wembley Stadium in a coach full of family and friends. Bristol Rovers were playing Grimsby Town with the winners gaining automatic promotion. The game was deadlocked at 1-1 after extra-time and so it came down to the dreaded penalty shoot-out.

Everyone around me stood up, fuelled by the excitement. But I just sat, somehow confident we were going to win. Moments later, everyone around me was going crazy as we won the shoot-out 5-4. I stayed sitting with tears in my eyes. I just knew we were destined to win. Ben always believed that winning at Wembley was the most exciting and best way of gaining promotion, so it was great that we did it that way. It was, after all, dedicated to him.

We finally received the decision we had been desperately waiting to hear – the parish council and local church granted us permission to plant a tree and install a memorial bench in remembrance of Ben on the village green at North Road in Stoke Gifford, opposite St Michael's Church. It was to be in a unique position in a pivotal part of the village. Just over the road is the Beaufort Arms and across the green is the welcoming church, which also boats a delightful café. We were so grateful to hear the decision went in our favour. Now we could plan a service to unveil the bench and tree, which would watch over Ben's ashes.

So many people kindly donated money to a fundraising account Rachel had set up which would help cover the cost of the bench. We would look to cover the cost of the tree and the installation work ourselves – especially as with his own landscaping and gardening business, Mike would see to this. It was our way of keeping it in the family.

More cruel and sad news came on July 1 when Jamie West's sister Georgina lost her fight against illness. Like so many others, our very deepest thoughts and sympathy were with Jamie and all his family.

Former Bristol Rovers and Liverpool player Nick Tanner introduced a new sport to Bristol on July 5 and, on behalf of Ben, dedicated some of the proceeds to Zoe and Aaliyah. The "footgolf" launch was a new game played around a golf course using a football instead of a golf ball. It had to be kicked from the tee until it went down an enlarged hole on the green. Many local celebrities from Rovers and City turned out to support the event, which proved popular and helped raise hundreds of pounds.

On July 7 I was at the Avon Coroner's Court near Bristol, along with lots of press and media, as we waited to hear the outcome of the inquest into Ben's death, which had started on April 22. The coroner's jurisdiction and duty is to look at and consider the circumstances surrounding sudden or unexpected death. Should anything arise that he thinks needs immediate attention and could prevent further deaths, he can enquire further into issues as well as writing to the authorities, asking them to take account of his findings.

The coroner confirmed that the distance between the goal-line and the clubhouse wall breached the FA's recommended safety guidelines, thus putting players at risk of death or severe injury. Considering there is also a slope on the pitch in the direction of the clubhouse wall which enables players to gain even greater pace, it has to be classed as a death trap. Further conclusive evidence came about when it was revealed that only a couple of seasons before, an identical incident happened on the same pitch in virtually the same spot.

Chris King was playing for Downend Foresters against Stoke Gifford when, like Ben, he went sprinting off down the wing in full flight. He too attempted to cross the ball just as it reached the goal-line and a nudge was enough to send him flying through the air, crashing against the clubhouse wall with his back. Chris was rushed to hospital and later forced to use crutches, but thankfully he survived.

In his final summing up, the coroner delivered a verdict of accidental death but confirmed he would be exercising his right to jurisdiction for the prevention of further deaths by writing to the FA, the club and the parish council drawing the circumstances of Ben's death to their attention. He confirmed that they needed to re-examine and if necessary move the pitch from its current position because, with the clubhouse wall breaching safety guidelines, action must be taken to ensure the pitch is made safe. He concluded by saying: "If a 30-year-old goes out playing football you expect them to come home in the afternoon and I would hate to think that this could happen to anyone else."

As a family we strongly support Stoke Gifford FC. But changes must be made to prevent horrific situations like ours from ever happening again. Nobody deserves to go through the hell that we have.

Arrangements had now been finalised for Ben's memorial at the village green on Saturday, August 1. Mike had managed to get the preparatory work finished so an apple blossom tree and the bench, which had a large dust sheet covering it, were in position ready for the unveiling.

The day before I had been along to the Radio Bristol studios to speak during their morning show. The aim was to make friends and others aware of the service and unveiling so they could attend if they wanted.

The following morning when we arrived, like many others, I parked in the Beaufort Arms car park. But as the others got out, I remained on my own for a moment of reflection. Ironically, it was the same parking space I'd used in my van that Saturday on March 28. It was here I spoke to a concerned Gloria on the phone, here where I watched three ambulances speeding past with lights flashing. Ben was inside one of them. Now, here I was sitting looking across the road. Fifteen metres in front of me stands the bench and the tree, awaiting the burial of his ashes. How cruel.

The number of people who turned up for the service was amazing. The Gifford lads were involved in a football tournament elsewhere, but they came back in full kit especially to attend the service before going back to the tournament afterwards. Simon Jones, the vicar of St Michael's, was ready and waiting to carry out the service and I was ready to put the ashes under the apple blossom tree, but first an urgent matter needed addressing.

The Gifford boys were not doing very well at the tournament – in fact, they were on the verge of being knocked out – so I met them all in the Beaufort Arms. I then placed the casket containing Ben's ashes on the floor. We all gathered around it and had a group hug while I said a few words of wisdom on behalf of Ben.

After that, it was straight over the road for the service. Simon carried it out to perfection. He chose and spoke his words solemnly. Everyone around remained silent – not just out of respect. They didn't want to miss a word he was saying. Shortly afterwards I positioned the casket under one side of the tree and then it was time to unveil the bench, which Gloria and I did to a tremendous reception.

As the service finally came to an end, Gloria finished it the only way she knew how. She stood there alone and started singing *Goodnight Irene*. I stood up to join her, Rachel and Mike were next, followed by Zoe, John, Lee and Wayne. Soon nearly everyone was joining in to finish the service the way it had started.

Later, although very emotional, Gloria and I sat down on the bench to reflect. The top rail of the bench bears the inscription: "Ben Hiscox, A Legend In His Lifetime, In Our Hearts Forever, 1984-2015." Along the bottom rail is inscribed: "I'll See You In My Dreams."

We are so grateful to have laid him to rest in this beautiful spot. After all, this is the village where he belongs. This is his village.

Young villager and good friend Arie Johansen said a few words on behalf of the village and summed it up perfectly. He declared: "Ben, your legacy lives on. Long live the king of the village!"

Later that day the Gifford lads returned triumphant. They had won the tournament on penalties (sounds familiar).

Ben had such an army of friends. He was part of the family to most and now each and every one could come and sit on the bench to reminisce over the good times they spent together. Not without a big smile, of course. Ben would not have it any other way. This young man had a unique ability to make a lasting impression on all who knew him. He was, after all, everyone's best mate who never failed to put a smile on all our faces.

On October 22, as a family we attended the Bristol Post Sports Awards held at the Marriott Hotel in the city centre. There were 14 awards to honour Bristol's sporting heroes, and Ben had been nominated for the footballer of the year award. Former England and British Lions rugby player Gareth Chilcott was guest speaker and presented the awards. When he came to footballer of the year and announced the winner was Ben, the whole room erupted. Every person around every table stood up, cheered and applauded as our family took to the stage to receive the award. After gratefully accepting the recognition, I said we were the proudest family in Bristol – and believe me, we were.

The applause continued until we returned to our table to sit down. To say the moment was humbling is a huge understatement. As the evening drew on, countless numbers of people came over to congratulate us. The love and respect shown by everyone was so gratefully received.

As the youngest member, Ben will always be the baby of our family and life will never, ever be the same without him. He really was a genuinely lovable character who never spoke ill of anyone or had a bad bone in his body.

Sometimes, when I'm alone, I reflect on things in general and curse our cruel luck. Why couldn't it have been me instead? Surely at my age, that would be fairer and makes more sense.

My mind then drifts back to the words my dad would say when I was a child if he heard any moans of self-pity. He always reminded us there were lots of people in the world a lot less well off than we were – and, of course, he was absolutely right. "Count your blessings," he would say. "You are one of the lucky ones."

So how do you define luck? Well, if you consider I have a beautiful family and a beautiful soulmate of a wife. Add to that I was able to share – along with so many others – the absolute pleasure of a kind, loving, humorous, legend of a son. So how fortunate is that! In terms of wealth, no amount of money could ever compare to it. Fortune? Millionaire? Ha ha! No thanks. I'm so grateful for what I had and what I have still got.

LUCKY, LUCKY ME!

TRIBUTES

Zoe Matthews

I never thought I would ever have to write anything like this. It all still seems so surreal. But I'm going to start at the beginning – our very first date at the good old Cider Press in Gloucester Road.

In our eyes, this was perfect from the start. I got blind drunk and you not only had to walk me home but plonk me on my sofa and leave me to sleep it off. When I woke up and the dreaded embarrassment hit me, I genuinely thought that would be it. But oh no, you kept coming back. Every single day, to be precise. You blew me away instantly after you met Aaliyah. You both got on so well.

It's no secret that we rushed into everything. We threw ourselves in at the deep end, but weirdly we both knew we wouldn't drown. You loved me and Aaliyah and we loved you. It was as simple as that. Along with all our happiness came friendship with others – you with my friends, me with yours.

Also came family, and for me that really was the icing on the cake. I cannot thank you enough for sharing your amazing family with us. I keep trying to be positive for Aaliyah by telling her to remember what else came with having you in our lives. I've never met a family quite like yours and I'll never let them go.

I love you for giving your heart to me and trusting me with your pride. I love you for the emotions I never thought I had. I love you for finding that part of me I never thought I'd find. I miss so much the little things about our lives together.

The bond between you and Aaliyah will always stick in my mind and that's the hardest part for me to come to terms with. How cruel and unfair that you are now gone. One morning in the hospital you were confused and looking for Aaliyah. You would not settle until the nurses told you she was safe at home with me. My last promise to you is to keep her safe forever.

I will shower her with enough love from both of us and she will never forget you. What a man you were to take on such responsibility and do it so well. You are the one for me and you are the one for Aaliyah. It took a long time to find you and, as I'm sure you know, we were never going to let you go.

I am going to end with our family holiday, which was only a week before you left us. What a trip! I have never believed in fate, but I believe that holiday at that time was meant to be. I remember standing outside the cottage on my own one evening having a sneaky cigarette. I was thinking: "Wow, this is it for me now. Everything I have ever wished for is sitting right inside. This is the happiest I have ever been."

Just like the rest of the family, I will treasure those memories for the rest of my life. What was supposed to be the first of many family holidays ended up being the last. I hope that wherever you are, you are peaceful. I need to believe that you are.

For the record, the answer to the question you were planning to ask me would have been, without any shadow of doubt, a big, fat yes. Thanks for changing my world for the better. Thanks for being not only my best friend but Aaliyah's too. Thanks for loving us so much. We will never forget and we will never let go.

Tim Walsh

I only really knew Ben when he was a child. It's only when tragic events like his death actually happen that you wished you'd kept in contact. You never think things like this would ever happen.

Stuart Ellison

I didn't know Ben in his adult years but it sounds like Ben the adult was no different to the Ben I knew as a child, which says a lot about the man he turned out to be. I wish I had known Ben the man. It sounds like he never really changed from being the type of friend we all seek and need.

Gary Warren

The thing that will always stay with me is Ben's massive cheesy grin and his way of charming anyone, no matter who you were. He always had nice things to say about you. He was humble and generous. I am so thankful that we met and became best mates because he played a massive part in my childhood. I'll forever miss you, mate. You were special to so many people. You will never be forgotten and are always in all of our thoughts.

Gemma Fisher

I don't know why, but every time I hear Coldplay's *Sky Full Of Stars* it reminds me of Ben. It makes me just sit for a few minutes and think of the fun times we shared growing up together. Sometimes a tear would fall, sometimes a massive smile. My memories of time spent with Ben are special ones that I will never forget. He was a pleasure to know.

Neil Whalen

Ben wasn't just a talented athlete but the most genuine person I have ever had the pleasure of knowing. He will be sadly missed in our family but never forgotten. He will always be in our hearts and memories. There is only one Ben Hiscox.

Lawrence Benson

Baz Luhrmann wrote: "Understand that friends come and go, but a precious few you should hold on." Ben really was one of the precious few. Bob Dylan said: "Take care of all your memories for you cannot relive them." I will miss you buddy. Rest in peace, my friend.

Rick Johansen

The king of our village – Stoke Gifford – was, is and always will be Ben Hiscox. At least twice every day I go past the bench and the tree. I love the bench. It overlooks the pub, the beating heart of our village where so many times I would bump into Ben and his legion of friends.

The tree behind the bench is usually adorned with beautiful flowers resting above Ben's ashes. It represents the continuation of life. It keeps alive the memory and sustains the spirit of Ben Hiscox.

It is right that we will always mourn Ben's passing but I also know a lot of people, especially the family, would like to celebrate this young man's life. Never have I known a man unite a village like Ben Hiscox. We all have many more friends than we did before and it has been a huge honour to get to know the close family, to become friends with them and so many others who before were acquaintances. He has bequeathed to the village an incredible legacy.

Lightning Source UK Ltd.
Milton Keynes UK
UKOW04f0305250717
305977UK00001B/73/P